College Basketball and Life's Greatest Lesson

College Basketball and Life's Greatest Lesson

By Brennan J. Bennett

For Sarah –

The girl who holds my world in a paper cup.
Thank you for opening your heart to the boy
in the painted jeans.

Contents

PART I: BOSTON COLLEGE

"The time you won your town the race
We chaired you through the market-place;
Man and boy stood cheering by,
And home we brought you shoulder-high.

To-day, the road all runners come,
Shoulder-high we bring you home,
And set you at your threshold down,
Townsman of a stiller town.

Smart lad, to slip betimes away
From fields were glory does not stay
And early though the laurel grows
It withers quicker than the rose..."

- A.E. Housman, "To an Athlete Dying Young"

"Some guys they just give up living
And start dying little by little, piece by piece,
Some guys come home from work and wash up,
And go racin' in the street."

- Bruce Springsteen, "Racing in the Street"

Chapter I

A Life-Long Love

"Even when I'm old and gray, I won't be able to play it,
but I'll still love the game."

- Michael Jordan

You look around at the home you have come to know so well. The sound becomes deafening – so loud that it seems to grow quieter by the second. It is a sound so familiar; it becomes the soothing lullaby of your mother, rocking you to sleep in her lap. This is the moment – the culmination of every day, every minute, every moment you spent loving it so ardently.

You are alone there – the most alone you can ever feel. You are on a desert island; you are in a wide-open field; you are alone.

You look left. You can see their loyal eyes; their moving lips producing no sound, their relentless passion gripping their hands into prayers of hope, and yet, you are alone.

You look right. You can see their hateful glares; their constant jeering seems to fall into the silent void you have created; their own relentless passion gripping their hands into tight, spiteful fists, and still, you are alone.

You can now see the faces of your teammates, their eyes filled with faith – the kind of faith that brings your heart to raptures and allows you to soar to heights previously unreachable and unimaginable. They are your soldiers, and you are their general. You have earned their trust, their faith, from years of leadership. Now this faith resonates from each of their unwavering expressions. Again, you clear your mind – remove all sensory perceptions. You are alone here.

Back further than you can seem to recall you have always loved it. Great portions of your early childhood were given for this love.

Countless hours, countless days spent slaving away, honing your skill, becoming the best you could be. Buckets of sweat shed for this and a limitless number of shoes sacrificed for it. You always knew it was worth it when you stepped onto the court.

As a child, you loved the sounds and smells of the gym. The rubbery texture of the floor was as normal and soft and welcoming as your own pillow. The empty bleachers were the four intimate walls of your room. Banners of heroes past and immortal teams of decades gone by hanging from the rafters were the posters of bands and singers that you did not have, and did not want. The whistle and whine of the shoes on the floor always gave you goose bumps, making the hair on your arms stand up in that gratifying way. And the pleasantly dingy aroma of sweat and hard work was always more appealing than the vivid fragrances of a Thanksgiving dinner. You and the game were best friends, stuck together until the end. You watched your heroes on television, aspiring to be just like them, even donning their names and talents in your backyard battles with yourself.

You toe the line, it laying snuggly beneath your feet in its all-too-familiar place. You don't even have to look down to know precisely where you are. Your mind is at ease. The silently deafening void seems to surround you, coming down upon you and leaving you utterly alone. The referee, his black and white stripes shining brighter than ever with the magnitude of this game, throws you the ball. It is almost as if the ball was made for your hand. Your heartbeat is calm, regular.

As you grew older, the two of you became inseparable. Wherever you went, it seemed to follow. When your mother took you along shopping with her, you brought it along, too. If you could not bounce the ball in the store, you would not go in, but rather stand outside, keeping loyal to your companion. For years your mother yelled, "Stop bouncing that goddamn ball in the house!" coupled by the typical, "Will you knock off that racket!?" However, to you, it never seemed like a racket, but rather, a soothing assuagement comparable to what many think of Beethoven's classical music (and you, of course, continued to do it). You knew every inch of its smooth exterior. You knew how it bounced, how it felt, and how it smelled. While other kids clung tightly to a teddy bear throughout the night, you slept only next to this extension of your hand. While the soft velvet of a stuffed animal soothed some children, the 9,342,059 individual bumps on the basketball were all the soothing you would ever need.

It is almost as if you are alone in an empty gym. The fact that there are thousands of people watching you, each one holding his breath, anxiously awaiting your result, doesn't faze you. Not even the astounding reality that *half* of the people in the gym are hoping you fail deters you from your dream. You stand on that familiar line; you dribble the ball once, twice, three times. The crowd seems to remain silent still, even in this moment of crescendo. You are alone. You are alone. You are alone.

You can remember a time when you almost lost the love forever. You toed the line, received the ball, heard the crowd, dribbled, and shot...and missed. This was one of the first times in your life where you met with such failure. All of the years of hard work seemed to sprout wings and fly out an open window, leaving you forever. From that time on, you vowed to never miss again. You would be perfect, or you would not be at all.

You are alone. You are alone. You can see the basket now. You are back in the empty gym. Just like you have done millions and millions of times before, you release the ball, poetically, dramatically, naturally. You know the results. Never for a minute did you doubt yourself. The ball crawls into the basket as if that is its only possible destination. At that incredible instant, the sound returns to the gym, like floodwater crashing over the breached walls of a withering dike. This is the blissful hysteria that you have waited your entire life for. The culmination of your years of hard work reach their climactic end as you and your men embrace passionately in the center of the court, overcome with exaltation, weeping as if you are men who have caught just a glimpse of Heaven. Every instant of this lifetime love seemed to be forever worth it.

"And what now?" you ask yourself. For as long as you can remember you sought only this instant. For as long as you can remember, you worked tirelessly, perfecting your game to reach this exact high. But what now? Tomorrow in the paper, you may be a feature story. For weeks, you may be the discussion throughout the halls of the school. For months, small children will idolize you, donning *your* name and *your* talents in their own backyard battles. And for years to come, you and your men will remember the utter nirvana you felt on that particular day. Through the course of the rest of your life, however, there will always be other shots – some less important, and many far more important. And in the ever-essential pursuit of perfection, in that constant strive for excellence, you will always reach the highest highs if you just surround yourself with the passion and love you have for the simple game of basketball.

*****

The aforementioned story was life for me from the moment I picked up a basketball until the day I thought my career had ended after my senior year of high school. Up until this point, I was a one-way street, a one-trick pony, a one-lady man – and her spellbinding pseudonym was Spalding. We truly were inseparable, the game and I. I would play from the time school ended until long after the sun had tucked itself in –when I would be shooting purely on muscle memory. But the sun always seemed to shine when the game and I were together – even on the rainiest of days.

There was another lurking in the shadows all along, however, waiting for the perfect time to throw a wrench in my gears. As the game and I continued to grow together throughout the years, I realized I loved something else just as much as basketball – learning. Soon after my senior season was underway, I made the arduous decision that there is life after basketball. (I know, how young and naive I was!) I determined that an education – a truly encompassing education – would be the only crutch I would ever need to make it in this world. When I think back to the moment that I made that decision, I always remember a lyric written by the band Survivor that says, "So many times, it happens too fast. You change your passion for glory. Don't lose your grip on the dreams of the past. You must fight just to keep them alive." I look back on that decision – that single moment in time – as the point in my life when I changed my passion and gave up fighting for the dream that I had worked so hard for throughout my life – to play college basketball.

I determined that this would be my last season – the end of a career, the end of an era – and I tried to make the best of it. As the season rolled along, I tried to lead my team with grace, skill, and passion. I poured in almost 24 points a game, pulled down nearly 8 rebounds per contest, and handed out almost 6 assists each night, leading my men to a third straight league title. But, truthfully, what did all that mean? I led a team of high school basketball players to a Division II, Central Massachusetts, Southern Worcester County League title. So what? Life, I determined, was far more than this – far more than basketball, far more than playing a game.

Furthermore, I had developed intellectually into the valedictorian of my high school class, boasting a grade point average of 4.93, and trailing a suitcase full of academic awards and trophies. With my résumé, I realized that I would be able to attend an elite institution of higher learning, and like clockwork, a letter of acceptance from Boston College found my mailbox and bore my name. I don't think it even took a full hour for me to send the deposit to BC to reserve my spot in the incoming class of 2010.

My mother always says I am a very impulsive person, like my father. My witty teenaged response was always, "Yeah!? So what? What's wrong with knowing what you want?" Looking back – and mind you, hindsight is always 20/20 – I was a foolish kid. I wanted to go to Boston College for all the wrong reasons. People knew what it was. People knew how great it was. People knew I would be there. People would know how great I was. (Notice a pattern?) Some call it egotistical, some say arrogant, and still others have created a new classification – Bennett Syndrome – and truthfully, I am now an advocate of calling it this!

Now, not only was I thinking and acting rather irrationally, but I had also ignored so many other intangibles – the assets in life that transcend value as we know it. I had forgotten my friends, my home, and my family; I had forgotten basketball. (Now, at this point, you may be saying, "C'mon kid! It's college; it's part of life. It's time to grow up and move on with things!" And I would wholeheartedly agree 99 out of 100 times; however, I believe that when someone "moves on" strictly for the wrong reasons, as I did, it's irrational.) I had been offered a few basketball opportunities at local, Division III programs, but, as I stated,

I had already determined that academics and perhaps some intramural basketball at Boston College would sustain me, and rather haughtily declined any offers.

Oh, to come face to face with my 18-year-old self! *"What makes you better than anyone else? What makes you think people will care if you're at BC?"* Oh, to have been humble; to not have been tempted by academic status! But I suppose every man must make his own mistakes. I suppose every man must figure *it* out on his own – whatever *it* may be. I suppose every man must discern his very meaning of life by himself.

I suppose it's funny how things find a way of working themselves out. My elucidation came from a much unexpected source: a game of pick-up basketball at Boston College with former Heisman Trophy winner Doug Flutie and Men's Basketball Head Coach Al Skinner.

Chapter II

Occupational Psychosis

"You don't play against opponents.
You play against the game of basketball."

- Bob Knight

When you're a basketball player – or an athlete of any kind, for that matter – you know how "good" you are. A true athlete knows his talent, and more importantly, knows his limitations. I had always been told "the sky's the limit." Some even thought this was too low; perhaps there were no limits. I knew my limits, though. I knew no matter how well I played, no matter how hard I worked, no matter how much I dreamed, I could never play Division I basketball. This fact was simply irrefutable. This fact was modestly accepted.

My freshman year began, continued, and approached its end in a relatively mundane fashion. Each day consisted of much of the same: class, shoot, lift, sleep. I felt as empty as a person can feel. I felt as though the life had been ripped from me; my heart pilfered from my chest and locked away in a dungeon somewhere next to some beautiful princess. The worst part of my situation was that I knew what my problem was. I knew all-too-well the source of my emptiness. I knew without doubt where my beautiful princess was hiding alongside my heisted heart. I missed the game I had spent my life playing; I missed basketball.

It's funny, when you really think about it. Kenneth Burke, a preeminent rhetorical theorist of the 20th century, calls it *occupational psychosis*. He describes this idea as a condition when something – perhaps one's occupation, one's interests, or one's hobbies – completely engulf this person. According to Burke, individuals can rationalize moods, ideas, behaviors, and even ways of life that seem completely absurd to other people because they are so passionately absorbed by this one thing. For me, this one thing is, was, and will always be basketball. Basketball is what makes me happy. It is what picks me up when I am down. Basketball fills that void that life can create far too many times along its course. And to many, perhaps you, this seems silly. Some might think this is nonsensical, even absurd. I suppose that's just it. This is the one thing for me that has no concrete meaning, and yet, has all the meaning there is to have. By this, I simply mean that basketball is more than a game to me; it is more than a hobby; it is more than an activity to pass the time. I mean to say that it is all of these things and more – it is a way of life. Simply, it has no set meaning because it has *all* meanings.

I can remember the exact moment I decided I needed to transfer. It was November 16th, 2006. At perhaps the mid-way point of the first semester, I determined that not playing basketball would ultimately drive me to drink. I took some initiative and created an intramural basketball team, appropriately named "Hoosiers," in a desperate attempt to quell the fire burning inside me; to assuage the beast eating me away, whose ferocity, as I would come to learn, I was only scarcely aware of at this time. I collected nine of the more skilled players I could find and entered the intramural tournament. We easily won the tournament, finishing 6-0, and for our troubles, were awarded with "intramural champion" T-shirts, Boston College mugs, and a pair of Champion socks. I can remember standing at half court after our championship game; no confetti falling, no people cheering, no people even watching. I remember the feeling of aloneness creeping up my body, settling in my gut, taking hold of me in a grasp so tight I wasn't sure how to escape it. However, this feeling of being alone was far different from the comforting, even embracing feeling of being alone in an empty gym shooting foul shots. This new alone feeling was almost palpable, seemingly alive and vengefully strangling me to death. I tormentingly remember one of my teammates saying, "Well, I guess it's better than nothing." The caustically bitter reality of where I was, of what I was doing, truly began to set in, leaving an almost acerbic taste in my mouth. It was like sinking slowly into quicksand with no one around to hear you yell. It was like a bad dream in which no matter how much you scream, you simply cannot wake up. It was in that moment of utter free-fall that I knew I had to do something. Transferring somewhere to play basketball might just be the way to wake from my nightmare.

I can remember returning home to my dorm that night as confused as the day I was born. Hesitantly I called my mother and revealed to her the truth that had been eating at me for almost four months now. She told me that life's about moving upwards and onwards, that sometimes, to truly grow as a person, we have to give up the things that we hold most dearly. I remember crying to her, sobbing like a child not ready to part with his teddy. I told her that some things we just cannot give up; some things we love so fervently that they cradle us in an embrace not so unlike that of a mother. I remember hanging up the phone more convinced than ever of what I needed to do. I needed to leave Boston College and play basketball.

I can remember participating in a service trip during February 2007. It was a sort of "get-away" weekend for students to relax, meet some new people, and really express themselves outwardly when perhaps they wouldn't have before. It was aptly named "48 Hours" because its designed length was two full days – Saturday and Sunday – and needless to say, I was not happy about participating. (I had been forced by my parents into signing up for this adventure.)

I suppose I have always been a relatively anti-social person. Not to say I don't have or make friends, but rather, I just like to keep to myself. Perhaps I'm just shy. Either way, I was to spend 48 hours with 200 complete strangers, each of whom awkwardly trying to become the next's best friend. I just remember thinking about how perfect everything would be when I transferred to my new school.

The weekend was full of mindless socializing events, the kind of corny activities that make you gag deep in your throat and cast that "is this for real" look just to see if anyone else feels as stupid as you do. However, one activity truly stands out in my mind. We were in small groups of seven or eight people, answering a questionnaire about what our time spent at Boston College has meant to us. We were to answer the questions as truthfully as possible and the leaders of the retreat were going to mail us our responses at a later date. I really didn't care about the questionnaire, but rather, flipped it over to the blank backside, and wrote the phrase "YOU'RE ONE STEP CLOSER TO PLAYING BALL AGAIN, DON'T GIVE UP!" This simple expression would prove quite extraordinary in the subsequent months – something that would change my life forever.

Chapter III

A Recurring Dream

"Byron was dead! I thought the whole world was at an end.
I thought that everything was over and finished for
everyone – that nothing else mattered."

- Alfred, Lord Tennyson, upon hearing of Lord Byron's death

Have you ever had a recurring dream? Perhaps a recurring nightmare? It can be anything, as long as it is the same dream repeating itself over a long period of time. Most people find their recurring dreams and nightmares centering on the sensation of falling, nakedness in public places, failing a test, not being able to speak, or drowning. And like most dreams, the recurring variety has numerous interpretations. Now, personally, I always found these rather humorous - that is, until one attached itself to my mind's hip. Not surprisingly, my recurring dream focused on basketball, and also not surprisingly, I began having this dream right after the start of the first semester of my freshman year. Moreover, there was nothing dreamlike about this recurring monster - it was a nightmare if I've ever had one.

It's game day. I pack my gym bag and leave my dorm for my game. My dilemma, however, always extends from the fact that I am always running late in this dream. I get to the gym about 20 minutes before the game is scheduled to start and everyone on my team is already seated around the coach, in full uniform, listening to the pre-game speech. Frantic, I rummage through my bag to get my uniform, but to no avail - my uniform is never in the bag. Panicking, I fly from the locker room in a full sprint for my dorm. It is always that kind of sprint as if something is maliciously chasing me - perhaps some unseen demon. It's that kind of dream sprint where my eyes become blurred, perhaps by tears, perhaps by wind, perhaps even by sheer fright. Moreover, it is that kind of sprint that no matter how hard I push, no matter how ferociously I churn my legs, I cannot move quickly. It feels as though I am bounding across the moon and whatever is behind me will surely catch me. Eventually, after what feels like an hour, I reach my dorm and grab my jersey, which is always innocently resting on my bed. I throw it into my bag and bolt back to the locker room in the same useless fashion.

When I finally reach the locker room, I discover that my team is no longer there, but rather, they have made their way to the court to begin pre-game warm-ups. I throw my uniform on hurriedly and reach into my bag to find my shorts. Not surprisingly, my shorts are incomprehensibly absent. My dream continues on much in this same fashion. The next time I return to the gym, my team has begun the game. This time, however, I find that my shoes are gone. The next time I return to the game, the second half is underway, and I find something else that has gone missing. Ultimately, I end up missing my entire game.

But what does this all mean? For quite some time I couldn't decipher the meaning of my madness. I felt violated; even in my subconscious I couldn't escape my yearning for the game. Then suddenly, it all became clear to me. The meaning of my nightmarish torment revealed itself through a song. I had been listening to a song called "Time is Running Out," by Papa Roach, and I felt as though the lyrics were written for me. The words go like this:

> "So I'm out of control, and I'm out of my mind.
> Just remember one thing, I think I'm just fine.
> So catch me when I fall, I won't remember anything at all.
> So catch me when I fall...
>
> When its time to fill the void, my whole life has been destroyed.
> And everyone around me says my time is running out.
> I refuse to surrender, I refuse to surrender..."

I felt like this song summed up my dream pretty well. I simply thought time was running out. I was watching my basketball career end before my eyes, watching it slip through my fingers like sand falling through a sieve. To a certain degree, time truly was running out. Moreover, I felt that if any more time were wasted, I would be like

Tennyson; I would feel as if the one thing that made life worth living – basketball in my case, Byron in his – would be dead and my world would be lost!

In stark contrast to my aforementioned impression of violation, I now felt as free as a bird. I felt as though I were French scholar Jean-Francois Champollion unlocking the door to Egyptian hieroglyphics with the help of the Rosetta stone! In this moment of clarity, I felt like my unrestrained free-fall had become a gentle coast through the clouds. My inexplicable incubus proved rather simply explained in the end. Other than spotlighting the demon behind my torment, deciphering this dream provided me with what I needed to do – I needed to begin the transfer process. While I had been almost certain that I needed to transfer before, after this moment of clarity, I no longer had even the slightest doubt.

*****

When I finally retuned home from that Hell on Earth which was formally known as 48 Hours, I began the transfer process – one I knew would not be short or easy. The first thing I did was create a spreadsheet of all the potential colleges I would or could transfer to. I can remember compiling a list of six schools – Williams College, Tufts University, Wesleyan University, Connecticut College, Middlebury College, and Trinity College – each one chosen based on its educational and basketball potentials. At this point in time, I still feel as though I was quite egotistical – far too caught on what others would think of me. I knew these six schools were some of the best schools in the nation educationally, as well as ones that would give me the opportunity to play Division III basketball at a very high level. Now, don't get me wrong, I understand the value of an education, and there is certainly nothing wrong with wanting to go to some of the best schools in the country. However, the reasons I had for wanting to go to them were strictly impure – similar to how I felt about Boston College. I wanted to attend these colleges because of their names, their reputations, but more than anything, because like at BC, people would know where I was and how well I was doing.

I remember compiling the spreadsheet – making basketball-related headings along the lines of "Record," "Number of Graduating Seniors," "Guards," and "Potential" (potential being a one through five star system). The spreadsheet took me a while to compile and when I completed it, I decided that Middlebury College, in Vermont, or Wesleyan University, in Connecticut, were the two most optimal choices, and fortunately for me, I was granted admission to each institution. After receiving my financial aid packages, I decided that Middlebury College was the right fit – and truthfully, the fact that I was the only transfer student admitted for the fall 2007 semester only boosted my already inflated ego, and certainly factored into my decision. With my transfer spot secure and my $40,000+ financial aid package in hand, I was off to attend Middlebury College; everything was finally perfect. However, as I have already discussed, things rarely work the way we plan.

Chapter IV

Two Loves

"With eight seconds left in overtime, she's on your mind.
She's on your mind."

- The Fray, "Over my Head (Cable Car)"

Here I must make a confession to my reader because I have not been totally honest to this point in my narrative. I have apprised my reader quite substantially regarding my true loves for the game of basketball and the pursuit of knowledge; however, what I have not yet delved into is my other love; a love that *truly can* bring one's heart to raptures - the love of a woman.

During my senior year of high school, having just 17 years under my belt, I met a girl named Sarah Oosterman. The first time I met Sarah, I actually had a steady girlfriend, whom I had been dating for more than three years - a girl whom I thought I loved. Looking back on those times, I suppose I can definitively say that I really did love Holly. However, it was a premature love - an immature love. I loved her because I thought I was supposed to love her. After all, we had been together for more than three years; shouldn't one love his girlfriend when their lives have become that intertwined? Perhaps it wasn't our love that was immature; rather, perhaps it was just I who was immature. I can remember fights we'd have - fights that I'd cause and then be too proud to end. I think marking myself as immature would be nothing short of appropriate.

We broke up after more than three years in late February of 2006, and truthfully, I was devastated. I remember thinking that I never *wanted* to love again so my heart wouldn't ever have to feel that way another time. That all changed when I met Sarah.

I am only 20 years old; I was only 17 then. I am too young to have a drink of alcohol. I am too young to gamble at a casino. I am even too young to rent a golf cart at my local country club. I am not too young to love, however, for there is simply no age when the heart is *ready* to feel true love. It just does. And reader, I cannot even begin to tell you the infinite opinions I've heard regarding such a young love. *"You don't know what love is!" "You're far too young to say you're in love!" "You won't know what love is until you're older!"* But reader, what is love? What is love but a four-letter word? What is love but that which makes one's knees weak and one's heart melt when that significant other comes around – when just the thought of her surfaces in one's consciousness? What is love but a passionate longing to spend every waking moment with that significant other? Isn't love sinking into your lover's arms, not being able to move, and simply not wanting to? Isn't love just that utterly sickening feeling one gets in the pit of his stomach when he has the thought of not being able to spend forever with his true love? To borrow a line from Bryan Adams, isn't love being able to see your unborn children deep in her eyes when she captures your gaze? Reader, if all this is love, I have most certainly found it, and what an incomparable love I have been blessed with!

But the truth of the matter, unfortunately, is that I have two loves. In one hand a hold the love for my girlfriend, Sarah. In the other hand, I hold a different kind of love for my game, basketball. Each makes me happy in a different way. Never before in my life had I had to grapple with such an inconceivable dilemma – which love means more to me. Up until this point in my life, basketball truly was my only love. I held it in such high regard; I put it on its own shelf, high above anything else life could throw at me (even academics). But now...now, I suppose, there was a rival in town, someone I held up with the same regard as my beloved pastime – perhaps higher.

I remember telling Sarah of my intentions to attend Middlebury in the fall. Without actually knowing Sarah Oosterman, it is difficult to truly appreciate the way her eyes can lie; it is almost arduous to decipher the meanings of her looks. When she looks at me, it is like she is looking through me; rather, she is looking into me, into my mind, into my heart, maybe into my soul. It's as if she knows what I *want* to hear, and always says it. When I told her I'd be attending Middlebury, she looked at me with the biggest and greenest eyes I'd ever seen and simply said, "Okay."

Later that semester, in early April, we decided to take a drive up to Middlebury to "finalize" my decision, but to be honest, at that point I was pretty certain of everything. We made the almost five-hour drive, toured the breathtaking campus, and at the end of it all, went to the book store to buy the ever-popular back windshield sticker that parents like to put on their cars to show their friends how awesome their kid is. But what really stands out in my memory is the long drive home. For almost an hour of the trip no words were spoken and that overbearing, almost eerie silence loomed over our heads like a thick fog. The worst part of the silence, however, was that I knew precisely what was wrong, and I knew the terrible discussion that would soon follow, but what I didn't foresee was the difficult decision I would be forced to make.

The silence was soon broken by painful crying. She looked at me, her beautiful eyes full of tears, and for once, I didn't know what to say. I knew what she wanted to hear: *I will not transfer to Middlebury*. But moreover, I knew what I wanted: to play basketball again. I tried my best to console her, pulling the usual bullshit a guy tells his girl when a situation gets sticky: "It's only a few hours; I'll have a car and I'll be able to see you every now and then. There is nothing to worry about. *It's not that big a deal.*" The true question here, however, was who was I trying to convince – Sarah or myself?

I suppose I really do believe the love Sarah and I share is that kind of truly lasting passion. It never really occurred to me that distance would ever diminish what we had. So, to me, going to Vermont for three years didn't really present a problem. For her, however, every passing mile marker of Route 89 southbound represented another time I wouldn't be able to see her; each exit represented another moment we wouldn't be able to share; each white line of the rushing highway represented another obstacle between us – another chance for us to drift apart. Perhaps it was just her insecurities making her feel the way she did. Perhaps she was playing to the stereotypes of the difficulties of a long-distance relationship. Maybe I was just blind to my own insecurities because of my lust for basketball. Any way you slice the cake, that car ride was one of the worst, most emotionally draining experiences of my life, but what would surely be more draining would be the months that would follow, because I knew I would be transferring to Middlebury in the fall. What I couldn't predict, however, was the series of curveballs the ace of the staff called Life would soon throw at me.

Chapter V
What a "Call!"

"The only way of discovering the limits of the possible is to venture a little way past them into the impossible."

- Arthur C. Clarke, *Profiles of the Future*

Elucidation is the act of explaining that serves to clear up and cast light upon. As I mentioned before, my elucidation came from a much unexpected source: a game of pickup basketball with Doug Flutie and Coach Al Skinner. But the question I propose is perplexing: Is something really an elucidation when it creates even further confusion?

When I returned to Boston College later in that week, the first thing I did was prepare to send a $200 check to Middlebury to reserve my spot in the class of 2010 and my dorm. However, before mailing this deposit, I received a call from a family friend named Mike Clasby. Mr. Clasby is a man who actually both works at BC and lives only about a mile from my house in Whitinsville, MA. In drill-sergeant fashion, he drilled me about my decision to leave BC. He asked me if I knew that BC was one of the top 30 institutions in the nation. He asked me if I knew how much a degree from BC really means when you graduate. Most importantly, however, he asked why I would possibly want to leave. I told him that yes, I knew how good a school it is; yes, I knew how much the degree means; and finally, I told him that I needed to play basketball again. I told him it was a love – an obsession – occupying my waking thoughts, consuming my every dream. His response to this: "So play here."

The sincerity and conviction with which he spoke these words was almost enough to make me laugh out loud. I felt like saying, "Listen buddy, I am just south of 6' tall, I weigh 185 pounds soaking wet, I can't jump, I can't shoot, and you're talking about playing Division I basketball in the ACC!"

For those of you who might not know, Division I is the top-notch basketball in the country. The kids who play this basketball are the McDonald's All-Americans, the 6'10" guys who can dunk a ball in their sleep, the guys who can make a three-pointer like it is a lay-up, and the guys who can run and jump like lightening and make guys like me look like maple syrup – slow maple syrup for that matter. Moreover, there are several conferences across the nation ranging from the Big East, the Atlantic Ten, the Big Ten, the Big Twelve, the Pacific Ten, the South East Conference (SEC), and arguably the most competitive, highly talented conference, the Atlantic Coast Conference (ACC). Again, for those who might not readily know, the ACC is comprised of perennial powerhouses Duke and North Carolina, as well as Clemson, Florida State, Georgia Tech, Maryland, Miami, North Carolina State, Virginia Tech, Virginia, Wake Forest, and of course, my Boston College Eagles.

I don't think it is possible for me to truly allow my reader to discern the level of talent the players in this conference have. You can watch ACC basketball on television and you can see how competitive the games are. You can go to a game and get a nice feel for the intensity of the game. You could even shell out some cash and get a front row seat and possibly get a feel for the sounds and smells of the game. However, until you have run with these players, jumped with them, shot with them, and played with them, it is simply impossible to grasp the speed, athleticism, and strength this level of basketball commands.

Now reader, I don't want you to get me wrong – I am a very good basketball player. I am 6' tall, weigh 185 pounds, have impressive quickness, and I can make a shot, and this is certainly more than sufficient when playing Division II Central Massachusetts high school basketball. In this level of basketball, I was playing against 5'9" shooting guards whose quickness paled in comparison to my own and whose jump shots were nothing to write home about, and big guys whose height may have, in some strange occurrences, exceeded 6'5" and who may have been able to dunk once in a blue moon. However, in the ACC the parallels to my previous level of basketball are simply nonexistent. Now the shooting guards are 6'5", able to pull up and hit a jumper from anywhere on the court, so quick that if you blink you might lose them, and so athletic that they could dunk the ball with ease. The big men are now 6'11", some even eclipsing 7' in stature, unable *not* to dunk and able to block every shot that goes up. Quite simply, reader, it is almost a completely different game.

*****

By the end of my conversation with Mr. Clasby, my ears literally hurt; I believe the conversation lasted nearly 45 minutes. If you know Mr. Clasby, you would know that he is truly a conversationalist. In other words, the man loves to talk to people, and he does so quite well. What is more significant than my ears hurting, however, is that by the end of our conversation, my ego had ballooned to almost 10 times its usual over-inflated size. For 45 minutes he spoon-fed me my high school stats, his flattering opinions of my game, and just simply how good I could be with hard work. Now, reader, I think it is important for you to know that while I would consider myself confident at times, I do not enjoy hearing people sing my praises. I almost feel embarrassed when people tell me how "good" I am at something, and by the end of my phone call with Mr. Clasby, I felt quite uncomfortable. In almost a drastic effort to end the conversation, I agreed that I would "look into" playing for the Boston College Varsity team, knowing wholeheartedly that there would be no in depth investigation at all, perhaps rather something like when a mother tells her son there is no monster under the bed and flips up the covers just to show that she looked.

As I was about to hang up the phone, he questioned whether I had ever played with the team, and moreover, if I knew any of the guys on the team or the coaches. I informed him that I had never met any of them, nor had I ever played with them. He then told me of a lunch-time pick-up basketball game at the Plex (our student recreational complex at BC), which might be a nice chance to meet some of the coaches and/or players. I felt like I couldn't shake this guy – like nothing I could say to him would deter him from his mission, which was to get me to play in this damned game. Almost out of desperation to end the phone call, because mind you, I had class to get to, I told him I would go to the Plex and play in the game. He was like a kid in a candy store as his enthusiasm poured out my end of the phone. He told me he'd meet me at the Plex and we could work out a little and then play in the game. Little did I know that I had set in motion what would truly be a life-altering experience – that this phone call would begin the process that would change who I was forever.

Chapter VI

"Picking Up" the Pieces

"Basketball doesn't build character; it reveals it."

- Unknown Author

I remember it was raining hard that April day and my ankle was hurting me. During my senior year of high school, as the premier wide receiver on the football team, I made an over the shoulder catch and was dragged down from behind, rolling my ankle over severely. After my x-ray, I was told that there was no break, but rather, just a bad sprain, leaving me sidelined for almost five weeks. To this day, when the weather is cold and rainy, my ankle still feels weak and frail when I put pressure on it. And on that particular day, the rain was making my ankle act up, and any athlete knows discomfort is never good when you're trying to make an impression on someone.

Likewise, I can vividly recall the sights and sounds of that day. I can remember how the gym looked - poorly lit, dirty, almost musty like dirt was falling down from overhead the courts (there are five courts at the Plex), sheeting them in a blanket of dust. I can remember the way the gym smelled - pungently bitter, salty even. I remember how the gym felt - overly hot and dry in some places, but at the same time, strangely dank and moist in others. When I first walked in, it was like a sauna, dry and oppressive, but after I began to run, it became unpleasantly moist, to the point where everyone's perspiration became almost palpable, like I could taste my own sweat, and no matter how much I needed a deep, fresh breath, the only sensation that would fill my nostrils was that of musty sweat.

I was a bit early, so I began to shoot a little on my own to warm up. At this point in time, I was 19 years old, and for many people out there, perhaps you, 19 seems young, like I haven't even begun to climb "the hill" yet. However, to me, I feel like an old man sometimes. I remember being 12 and 13 years old and just being able to go outside and run and jump and play. However, now, being the old man that I feel I am, if I don't first warm up with a light jog, then spend a solid 10 minutes stretching before I begin to really play, it will not be a pretty sight. At first, I will resemble the Tin Man from *The Wizard of Oz* – stiff, inflexible, and rigid – and this rigidity will certainly and inevitably lead down the familiar road to a pulled muscle.

After I did my warm-up routine, Mr. Clasby arrived, ready to put me to work. We started with some light shooting; I had to make 10 shots from six different spots on the floor (baseline, wing, elbow, elbow, wing, baseline) and then repeat the same process from three-point range. Now, this is not an overly tiring drill, but when someone is pushing you aggressively the entire time, it can become a bit fatiguing. However, what truly did me in was the one-on-one game he forced me to play following my shooting. He made me put up a shot, and if I missed, get around him (he was boxing me out), get the ball, and lay it up – and we did this about 10 times. Needless to say, by the end of the tenth round, I was pretty gassed (at this point in time, I was nowhere near basketball shape). Also needless to say, due to the Bennett Curse (which is self-explanatory), the guys involved with the pick-up game decided this exact moment would be the optimal time to walk in and start the game. So, after narrowly avoiding tripping over my tongue, which was awkwardly hanging out of my mouth and dangling near my feet due to exhaustion, I walked over to the guys and introduced myself.

I was actually surprised to discover that most of the guys who were playing were older men, most between the ages of 30 and 50. I recognized a few of the guys, a couple of professors and people who worked at the university. I was star struck to discover that former Heisman Trophy winner and professional football player, actually a former New England Patriot, Doug Flutie was also among the group (and to my surprise, he was quite a basketball player as well!). I remember being nervous to introduce myself to him; so naturally, I donned that "deer in the headlights" look, and with a dry mouth, muttered an inaudible, "Hi, I'm Brennan." Furthermore, I wasn't sure what to call him. Doug? Mr. Flutie? To avoid the potential awkwardness of that situation, I just avoided calling him anything at all. I suppose that is just my shyness at its best. Actually, after getting to know Doug Flutie, I determined that he is a very nice guy. He was friendly and spoke with me as if I were a celebrity like him. I remember him telling me that he had just gotten back from a Super bowl party with Peyton Manning (at that point in time, the Indianapolis Colts had just won the Super bowl. And for the record, it pains me to say that, and I will never refer to that again). It just impressed me that a person of his celebrity would take the time out of his own schedule to play in a pick-up basketball game with a kid like me. Perhaps he just likes to give back to the school that gave so much to him. Needless to say, I was extremely impressed with the overall character of Mr. Flutie.

Also to my surprise, Coach Al Skinner was among the group, so I took special pride when introducing myself to him, trying not to have that shy, star struck appearance with him, too. Truthfully, I don't know what I expected. I wanted him to see me play and just to say, "C'mon! You can join the team tomorrow!" However, at the same time, I knew this was not only impractical, but improbable, and moreover, impossible.

We made teams and started the game. I noticed a kid on the other team that looked like he was probably on the team, so I figured, if I'm going to impress Coach Skinner, I should try to shut down one of his scholarship players.

For the first few possessions, I decided to try to play him tight defensively, meaning I would only leave about an arm's length of space between him and me when he had the ball. I have always considered myself a superior defender and one of my strengths as a basketball player is never getting "beaten in my yard" – the three feet extending in either direction, horizontally, from my body. Each time he caught the ball on the wing, I'd close the gap to arm's length, but with quickness and strength unparalleled by my competition in suburban Central Massachusetts Division II high school basketball, he'd blow by me with an arsenal of basketball moves, the likes of which I had never even imagined. He had a repertoire complete with "killer" cross-overs, spin moves to create space, and a first step like lightening – one, much to my dismay, made my own look like a Model T Ford next to a NASCAR speedster.

That game was probably the longest pick-up game of my life. As I mentioned, I was dragging my feet before we even started playing, and right from the "get-go," my legs felt like lead; they felt like anchors strapping me to the ground and not allowing me to stay in front of this kid.

In addition to considering myself a superior defender (something that was now under some serious internal scrutiny), I've always thought myself to be an extremely intelligent ballplayer – something of a "floor general." In other words, I usually know what to do at certain points in a game and more importantly, what not to do at certain points in a game. I constantly look for ways to adjust my game to offer me the greatest advantage possible, and subsequently, the greatest advantage possible for my team. In an attempt to even the playing field against this kid – to decrease the monstrous gap between his quickness and my seeming lack there of, I made a defensive adjustment and decided to back off him a bit, now giving him about six feet on the catch. This way, I would force him to make a jump shot to beat me, because if he tried to drive to the basket, I would have those six feet to react to his first step and close the driving lane. Unfortunately for me, this type of defensive strategy hinges on one important factor – that the offensive player cannot consistently make a 15-20 foot jumper, and in this case, the jump shot was this kid's most dangerous weapon. He effortlessly stroked four consecutive catch-and-shoot jumpers and then, as if letting me know I was nothing more than the mouse to his cat, he, on his next offensive series, caught the ball on the wing, took one hard dribble toward the basket, pulled up from the foul line like Jordan against the Cavaliers in '89, and released the ball, its destination never in doubt. With the evidence of the pull-up game in his repertoire, my defensive efforts were almost in vain – I wasn't going to stop him if there had been three of me guarding him.

Quite simply, it felt like an eternity before the other team finally scored their 21st point and the game was over. I suppose then, that it felt like two eternities before I got over to the water fountain, seeing as how I had to periodically stop and take in heaping gulps of oxygen.

I can't even truly describe my feelings at that moment in time. I felt sad. I felt depressed. I felt exhausted. I felt defeated. I felt like Keats' "sick eagle looking at the sky," unable to fly. I remember thinking to myself, as this kid took me to the basket time and time again and hit 15 foot jumpers with tremendous ease, maybe this isn't worth it; maybe I'm just not as good as I thought I was; maybe, I just loved the *idea* of playing basketball again. I didn't even stay to play a second game. I walked out of the gym with my tail between my legs like a beaten dog, embarrassed, almost as low as I'd ever been. I think this moment may have even eclipsed my other moment of great depression (after my intramural championship game) because now, after that day's debacle, I didn't even think playing Division III was feasible any longer - I thought, right there on that court, my last chance to play basketball had faded into nothingness, away from me forever.

*****

I got back to my dorm that night and sulked for hours - that kind of miserable sulking that makes everything, even the things that weren't bad before, seem as miserable as ever. I couldn't believe that kid wiped the floor with me the way he did; I just had never been beaten like that before on a basketball court in my entire career. I remember looking on the Boston College Athletics website, just to see if I could find out that kid's name - maybe he was the starting shooting guard, and in that case, I wouldn't feel so bad. When I looked down the picture roster, I was perplexed not to find the kid I had played against. Something did not add up. I knew it was not possible that the kid that I guarded - well, attempted to guard - was just an average student; he had to be on the basketball team. I continued looking at the roster, scrolling down the page slowly, and to my surprise, I found his picture at the bottom of the page. To my astonishment, this kid was not a kid at all, but an adult. In fact, this "kid" was a four-year letter-winner at the University of Rhode Island. In fact, this "kid" had played professional basketball over seas for three years in Belgium and Holland. In fact, this "kid" had played as a member of the Los Angeles Clippers in the NBA pro summer league! This "kid" was assistant coach for the Boston College Men's Basketball program, Preston Murphy!

After learning that I had had my rear end kicked by a former professional basketball player, I certainly didn't feel so miserable, and in fact, I began looking at it in a positive light. I decided then that I would go back to the gym the next day and play in that pick-up game again. I decided that if you want something bad enough, you have to fight to keep your head above the water – you have to fight just to keep your dreams alive. I went back to that game each and every day for the rest of the semester, and each and every day I walked away physically beaten, but each time I walked away a little better, a little wiser, and a little more confident. I now viewed the situation with almost peculiar optimism – peculiar in the sense that while I was still getting outplayed, I was getting better each day, and in my mind I felt like if I could now stay with a guy who was a former professional basketball player, I could certainly play with guys at the college level.

By the end of the semester, my skill-level had skyrocketed, my quickness had improved significantly, and my confidence had soared. Moreover, my deadline to send my money into Middlebury was fast approaching. I decided that while perhaps I was still not talented enough – maybe just not tall enough – to play Division I, I was certainly ready to play Division III, and confidently, I sent my $200 deposit to reserve my seat in the Middlebury College class of 2010. (Ultimately, despite the fact that I knew my decision would be extremely difficult on both Sarah and me, I decided that playing college basketball was important enough to me to attend Middlebury and endure the rigors of a long-distance relationship. I was confident that our love was strong enough to withstand anything.)

*****

The final week of the semester had finally come, and with it, a dreadful and ghastly set of final exams. Finals are awful; it's like you're looking at a police lineup where each face – or final in this case – is just a little worse than the one before it. As you move down the line, each one get's a little tougher, a little harder, and little more appalling. However, to my astonishment, finals didn't seem to bother me much that semester. Actually, if anything, I was just excited for summer to arrive so I could start my workout regimen and prepare myself for the next stage in my life – Middlebury.

Being the ever-studious scholar that I am, I *somehow* found time to engage in my daily pickup game, even in the midst of finals week. It's almost funny how "out-of-whack" my priorities were during that week. Instead of making time to study for finals, getting ample learning in, and then if I had time for basketball, playing for a while, I was the opposite way around. I would schedule my study times around my pickup games and my periodic afternoon shoot-arounds. And truthfully, I don't really have any way to rationalize my behavior, other than saying that when you love something the way I love this game, you almost look for ways to do it. I suppose I can cite rhetorical theorist Kenneth Burke again to help me with this rationale. He has an idea, very closely related to "occupational psychosis," called "terministic screen," which says that when you have some kind of occupational psychosis – a job, a hobby, or basketball in my case – you view it with a certain point of view – one that, in almost all cases, favors your psychosis substantially. In other words, this particular fascination will color your viewpoint, similar to that of a bull seeing the enraging red of a matador's cape. You will see only this, put it first in all cases, and certainly make it your number one priority – and that is just what I did.

I had sent my money into Middlebury College on the Monday of that week. On Tuesday, I had *mysteriously* found my way to the paradisiacal rubber floors of the Plex basketball courts – well, paradisiacal when compared to the agonizingly torture chamberesque locale of Boston College's Bapst Library.

On that particular Tuesday, the rest of the guys were a little late arriving for our game. I had been shooting by myself when I noticed Coach Skinner and Coach Murphy walk in followed by the usual tagalongs. On a typical day, they will arrive, talk among themselves for a while, ask me to join the game, pick teams, and begin. Neither coach is ever overly talkative in my direction, and I don't think, to this point, either of them had even addressed me by name! However, on that day, to my astonishment, Coach Murphy came right up to me, looked me in the eye, and asked me how my grades were. Shivering with confusion, I stood there in front of him, wrapped up in a blanket of nervousness and anxiousness, and I almost yelped at him, "3.92 GPA." Upon hearing my response, he looked as shocked as I must have looked prior to giving it. He looked almost perplexed, opened his mouth, and then everything froze...

It was one of those moments where I could honestly see everything around me, but nothing seemed to move. It was almost as if I could reach out and touch him and time would have still stood still. Suddenly, like a wave crashing violently to the shore, all of the sound rushed back into the room, and what he said would truly alter the course of my life and change every fiber of my being forever.

Chapter VII

A Unique Opportunity

"Holaqd fast to dreams, for if dreams die,
life is a broken-winged bird that cannot fly."

- Langston Hughes, "Dreams"

"Have you ever thought about playing for the team next season?" When the sounds came out of his mouth, I was left speechless – perhaps even flabbergasted. The question was like music to my ears. Each word forming this question was like a classical instrument and as they meshed together, they produced the truest harmony one's ears could ever hear; the words built upon each other, growing louder and louder, until I heard myself burst forth with the crescendo as I exclaimed, "Absolutely! I'd love to!"

I was overcome with jubilation. It was an exultation I'd never even begun to feel and one I truthfully never imagined I'd experience. I was warm, excited, anxious, nervous, and shocked all at the same time. I felt like I could fly to the moon just by pushing off the ground. I felt like I could run 100 miles, and then run back without breaking a sweat. I don't remember a single other thing that happened that day. I don't remember how I played in the pickup game, how I did on my final that day, or even how I got down from the top of the backboard (because that was how high I felt like I jumped when I learned of my new fortune!). All I can remember from that day is that feeling of utter bliss – that feeling of true accomplishment. However, what I didn't realize at this point in time was that this feeling was only a mirage; it was only an illusion hiding its true identity – its true ugly face – behind a smiling mask. But in the months to come, this cloaked intruder would undoubtedly show its hideous countenance, creating for me a void like no other – one that might be impossible to fill.

Chapter V

I am Passi

was my bedrock
however, this
false sense
altogeth
star

"Success is a journey, not a destination.
The doing is often more important than the outcome."

- Arthur Ashe

It's almost comical how quickly one can become wrapped up in his own greatness. We, as human beings, are almost comical in this way by our very nature. We have an uncanny ability to miss the big picture – to see ourselves not as how we really are, but rather, as we imagine others will see us. Take a minute to look in the mirror; how many times have you purchased something or done something just so others will make a comment about it – perhaps an article of clothing, perhaps a haircut, or even gone on a date with someone. However, what will truly bake your noodle is when you think about how many times you *haven't* done something because of the ramifications it would affect – and by ramifications, I assuredly mean nothing groundbreaking, simply what results will effectuate from those who formulate an opinion about you. How many times have you not asked a person out, not bought something you liked, or not eaten that piece of dessert because you concerned yourself more with what others have to say rather than what you yourself feel or want? What it all boils down to is this simple question I hope each and every person has the courage to ask themselves: How many times have you put your own happiness on the backburner in the pursuit of appeasing the faceless many? For me, the answer is *at least* one too many.

On Monday of that fateful week of final exams, I made my decision to attend Middlebury. I laid the framework of what I thought would be a house of the utmost sturdiness – one ripe with brawn; robust and stalwart, erected on the most resolute of foundations. Brick and happiness my mortar. On Tuesday of that week, all went by the wayside. I had become overcome with a of accomplishment. I had been swept away in the mighty and er persuasive current of the fast-flowing river of potential dom. I was going to play Division I basketball at BC. I was the ourth Little Pig, blinded by the stars in his eyes, who traded in his stout brick for feeble straws and who replaced his happiness-charged mortar with a frail yarn tie forged from the dying dreams of once-important stardom. My Big Bad Wolf would undoubtedly come; the only questions that remained were when and with what ferocity...

*****

After about a week of telling everyone I had ever known about my invitation to be a member of the Boston College Eagles basketball team – parents, siblings, friends, cousins, great aunts, grandparents, second cousins twice removed, third grade classmates whom I haven't seen in 10 years, etc. – and subsequently explaining to everyone that, "No, I am not making this up," I decided it would be best to speak with Preston Murphy more about the validity of my position. In fact, the more people who told me that I couldn't possibly be on the BC team, the more I started to believe them. After a weeklong game of telephone tag, I finally spoke with Preston and he invited my father and me to have a meeting with him the next day.

During our meeting with Preston, my father and I poured a barrage of questions onto Preston, who was most likely unprepared for the extreme level of inquiry. We asked questions like, "How sure are you that Brennan will be on the team?" or "Is there going to be a try-out?" or "Will Brennan be allowed to travel with the team?" (All right, so my father was asking most of the questions. Truth be told, I was still in shell-shock over the whole situation and I would have believed anything Preston said. He could have been trying to sell me a winter coat in Hell and I probably would have bought it hook-line-and-sinker.) Preston seemed to give all the "right" answers that day – "right" meaning the ones we needed to hear. He told me that I was going to be on the team, and that there was almost certainly not going to be a try-out – that my playing pick-up each day the last semester was try-out enough. He told me that I would have every benefit of being on the team that all the other guys had – I would travel, get a uniform, get shoes, etc. He did offer me one caveat, though. He told me that I would have to be a contributing member of the team, but that I should not hope to be rewarded with any playing time. He said that I might actually get no playing time the entire year.

I remember the look my father wore when Preston was giving us these admonitions. His face said *be careful and think this one through*, though his mouth said, "Ultimately, it's your call," but for me, it was literally a no-brainer. After all, is there anyone out there who would turn down a chance to play Division I college basketball in the ACC? (If there is, I'd like to meet him.) My father warned that perhaps playing Division I hoops would be an amazing experience, but he asked me if not playing come game time was something I was ready to deal with. After all, the reason I initially wanted to transfer schools was to *play* basketball – not to watch it with a front row seat. He wondered if my head might be making the decisions usually reserved for my heart. In other words, perhaps I was being a bit hasty or making this monumental, life-altering decision for the wrong reasons, and in fact, that was exactly what I was doing.

I have to be honest with myself and admit that I made this decision using what many people refer to as "fortune telling" or "crystal balling." I envisioned myself strutting through Lower Campus at BC showing off my black-on-black Boston College Basketball sweat suit, proudly displaying my number and therefore, my status as a member of the team. I imagined what people would think when they saw me wearing my jersey or when they saw me on television playing against Duke or North Carolina. I envisioned my friends and family coming to the games to watch me on some of the biggest stages in the sports world. And despite Preston's literal guarantee that I wouldn't see the court, I somehow held out this glimmer of hope that I would make it – that I would be able to convince my coaches and teammates that I actually belonged out on the court with the ball in my hands. It never crossed my mind to say no to Preston and Boston College Basketball, and despite my burning desire to get back on the court as a vital member of a team, I accepted the position as the walk-on of the Boston College Basketball program.

*****

I had officially decided to remain at Boston College despite the significant amount of obstacles I would assuredly face in the approaching semester. For a start, I had already sent my non-refundable deposit to Middlebury, so ultimately, I was out $200. Next, because of my one-time certainty surrounding my transfer, I had neglected to pick a roommate for the next year. During the second semester of my freshman year, I had been asked by my then-current roommate, John McMahon (who remains one of my good friends) if I wanted to live with him and six of our friends (including another one of my good friends, Nick Kodama) for sophomore year. Regretfully, I had to turn down their proposition, a choice I immediately began to deplore upon my decision to remain at BC. Ultimately, this would mean that I would not only miss out on living in the "better" upper classmen housing with my friends, but also, that I would be assigned a random roommate from the pool of singles. Truthfully, when you're awaiting to be assigned a single roommate, thoughts of sick-o's and axe murderers run through your mind. After all, why are they in the singles pool and not rooming with their own friends from freshman year? (It wasn't until later that it dawned on me that they were most likely thinking the very same thing about me!)

Moreover, I had also neglected to pick classes for my sophomore academic year. I didn't anticipate this to be an overly large problem, I would still most likely get the classes I desired; however, I would certainly be stuck with rotten times, i.e. 8 a.m. classes three times a week. Upon deciding that I would stay at BC, I immediately went to see my academic advisor to ask her opinion regarding my class schedule. She told me that all I could do was just pick my classes from the remaining class pool and unfortunately, hope for the best. Needless to say, I was rather disappointed and even a bit dismayed as I left my advisor's office that day. I had hoped that she would provide me with some override code that would let me pick any classes I wanted at any time I wanted; perhaps even a magic elixir that would make me impervious to the mistake I had made (that being not just picking classes for the hell of it in the small chance that I remained at BC). Quite literally, all I obtained from her was my access code (a code that I needed to punch into the system to allow me access to pick my classes), a shoddy "good luck," and a swift quick in the backside and out the door because her next appointment had arrived.

Looking back on it, I now realize that my advisor surely held no mysterious vendetta against me, rather, it must be difficult to be an academic advisor in a place like Boston College. There's just an incredible amount of people, each seeking the advice of a small number of advisors, and what it all boils down to is that there simply isn't enough time in the day to answer each and every person's questions about everything. That was one thing I always hated about being a student at BC - I always felt less like a person and more like a number. There were so many times when I would badly need assistance - from an advisor, from a dean, from whoever or whatever - and I just never felt like anyone really cared about me - like no one could ever take the time to help me. To BC, I was simply a dollar amount, and a significantly lower one than the majority of the other numbers/students.

With access code in hand, I drudged back to my room, mulling the whole way over both the lack of advice I had received and how in God's name I was going to assemble a remotely feasible schedule out of the scraps of classes the hyenas had left for me. After a solid hour of assembling and dissembling my schedule, I finally agreed with myself upon a schedule that could work -in other words, one that wasn't too horrible.

*****

The summer of 2007 came and went, and as it neared its end, I received my housing information for the upcoming year. As I had pessimistically predicted, I had, in fact, been assigned to the worst possible housing, a housing complex known as College Road. "Co Road," as it is called, is known to be so terrible because like all freshman dorms, Co Road also has traditional double rooms and a community bathroom on each floor, rather than the much-sought-after eight-man suite-style housing which the upper-classman housing offers. The proverbial icing on the cake came just a few minutes later when I learned my roommate, a kid named Andrew Cangemi, whom I had never met nor seen for that matter, was from Long Island, New York, and would undoubtedly be a New York sports fan (As difficult as that is to stomach, there are actually people out there who like New York sports.).

For anyone who doesn't know me well, I am quite the diehard Boston sports fan, literally bleeding Red Sox', Patriots', and Celtics' colors. I can't even describe the passion I have for my city's sports other than by saying that when they lose a game, my whole day is negatively affected. In fact, when my team loses, I go out of my way to avoid watching Sportscenter or reading a newspaper that might remind me of our shortcoming. I even form my daily schedule around scheduled sporting events, so as not to miss a minute of one. Now you may be thinking that these are just sports, only games played on television by over-paid oafs who don't know you or care about you in any way. If you were thinking this, well, you're exactly right, and I know that. What's even stranger is that for some reason, I allow differences in sports allegiances to have an effect on the way I view others and the way I form relationships with others. I would certainly try to like and get along with my new roommate, but unfortunately (and even ashamedly), I knew there would be a barrier between us, at least in my mind, before we even met for the first time. I suppose it's just one of my character flaws – a vice forged from the passion that undoubtedly forms my one true tragic flaw – my unwillingness to lose.

I want my reader to know the difficulty I faced when composing the end of this chapter. My relentless passion is something that, while I am not ashamed or embarrassed to have, does have a strong and strange effect on me. I would never say I was ashamed of the passion that drives me to excel in everything I do, but sometimes this passion spills over to things that, for lack of better words, aren't as important, i.e. professional sports. It is hard for me to admit that the thing that makes me the athlete, competitor, and even the person who I am, also makes me ugly in many instances. I suppose I will ultimately chalk up my undying passion as a "catch-22," because in the end, no real dilemma exists surrounding it. By this, I mean that while it has an effect on me, there is no choice to be made. I cannot choose to be passionate about anything; it is simply in my blood; it is my person and I am passion. (On a side note, Andy and I ended up being good friends despite the fact that he roots for the "bad guys.")

Chapter IX

Answer the Phone;
"Real" Life's Calling!

"You miss 100% of the shots you don't take."

- Wayne Gretzky

People always tell me how their college years were the best four years of their lives. *"You'll never get them back! Cherish them!"* The truth is, I've always been more of a summertime kind of guy. For me, nothing beats reclining on the beach, digging my toes into the sun-baked sand, feeling the warm rays of the sun dance across my face, and not having a single care in the world, other than what I'm going to get for lunch and whether or not the iPod will have enough battery life to make it through the entire Springsteen playlist (it never does!). What I cherish is feeling the stiff Vermont breeze caress my hair as I hike with my best friends – Sarah, Andrew, Smalls, Pipes, and Dobes - to our secret swimming hole which lies tucked away from the world, hiding in the side of a mountain. What I cherish is getting to see Sarah every single day, and not having to count down the days until the next time I get to see her for a transitory two hours. What I cherish is the summer!

The summer of 2007 was to be the best summer to date. All of my closest friends were home from their respective colleges for the summer, and it was to be like old times – poker, cigars, the drive-ins, the beach, Vermont, and a whole host of other things that Summer brings in her bag of treats. This particular summer, my sister Kelsey (who was 13-years-old at the time) had qualified for the national dance competition in Daytona Beach, Florida, and my mother was allowing Sarah and me to come along. The trip was truly amazing; it was relaxing and enjoyable to the utmost extent, but most of all, it was just carefree. Each and every ounce of stress, like a vice pressing and squeezing my mind for all it was worth, was cast away to the highest mountain or the lowest valley or anywhere other than Daytona Beach. The trip was one of those perfect getaways; but what I never saw coming was how the return trip would be even more memorable.

As we stood in the airport – barely recognizable when compared with how we looked when we left – displaying our hard-earned tans, spray-on tattoos, braided hair, and faces that screamed out our easygoing dispositions, my forgotten-about cell phone began to ring in my pocket. Not immediately recognizing the number responsible for this violent shove back into real life, I answered the call with an overly confident and almost agitated, "Hello." However, my once-abounding self-assurance melted into the eloquence one would assign to a bowl of Jell-O as the voice on the other line responded, "Ay yo, it's Tyrese Rice from Boston College Basketball."

*****

I will never forget the feeling that came over me when I received that phone call from Tyrese. I began to shake like the last faded leaf remaining on the late-autumn tree, clinging to the dear life of summer as winter's icy grip pulls it away with hurricane force winds. I must have stuttered wickedly and spoken quicker than an auctioneer talking his way out of a sticky situation, as well (I have always spoken quickly and stuttered a bit when I get nervous), but after I said hello, I found myself just doing most of the listening in the conversation. The whole thing just felt so surreal. Tyrese Rice, a big time college basketball star, was on the phone with me! This certainly must have been a dream, a figment of my imagination, or maybe I was just going nuts. After all, why would Tyrese Rice be calling me? I mean, I know Preston Murphy wanted me to try-out for the team, but wasn't a try-out supposed to be held in early fall, immediately before the commencement of the season itself? To my astonishment, Tyrese asked me if I wanted to come up to BC and play some pick-up basketball with him and the rest of the guys on the team (including the new freshmen, who had already been up at BC for almost the entire summer). He told me that they played pick-up Sundays, Tuesdays, Wednesday, and Thursdays, and that I was more than welcome to play if I felt like making the drive. I suppose looking back on that proposed question, it really was one of the questions that there can only be one answer for, like when your father asks if you'll take out the trash, or when your mother asks you to drive your sister somewhere. I mean, would you have me say no? I suppose the same infallible logic held true with the question Tyrese asked me that day as I stood elated in the airport wearing the grin of a six-year-old on Christmas morning across my face. I hope looking back on it, the quickness and enthusiasm with which I said, "Yes," and the way I probably screamed into the phone didn't scare him at all. I gathered, in the months that followed, however, that the enthusiasm of the walk-on really didn't matter much to Tyrese Rice, or any other members or coaches of the 2007-2008 Boston College Eagles. And as my enthusiasm would begin to expire in these same subsequent months, I would come to find myself making one of the most life-altering choices I could ever dream of, and in the process, discovering something that would change the way I looked at life forever.

Chapter X

History's Longest Journey

"There is no terror in a bang, only in the anticipation of it."

- Alfred Hitchcock

I returned home from my vacation on a Sunday night and decided without haste that I would make the drive to BC on the following Tuesday to play ball with the team. Of course, I wouldn't take part in a single bit of physical activity until I laced up my Reeboks and ran with the team simply because the Bennett Curse just wouldn't have allowed me to make it through any physical activity that Monday without turning an ankle or pulling a hamstring. Some things I just have to accept as truths in life – and the Bennett Curse is one of them. How else can you explain a baseball team going 86 years without winning a World Series? The most obvious explanation is that four generations of Bennetts had been cursing them, not this Bambino fellow everyone was so obsessed with. I suppose the World Series Championships in 2004 and 2007 just prove that I'm the least cursed of my family, though I wouldn't say "least cursed" is something I'd like to write home about or have inscribed on a medal. As aforestated, some things I just accept as truths.

The drive from my house in Central Massachusetts to Boston College proved to be the longest hour of my life to date. I'm relatively certain that at some point, the Massachusetts Turnpike must have sprouted legs as well as some wicked desire to spurn me, because I can't fathom how one highway can seem so utterly endless, unless, of course, it is walking under the wheels of my car, truly making itself longer with every mile! Many experts will suggest that it was just a simple cocktail of excitement and anxiety working against my mind, making the trip seem a million light-years long instead of just 30 miles, but I still think to this day that my personification of the Mass Pike is not totally out of the question. Either way, I felt like it took weeks upon weeks to finally spot the Tower on the Heights and pull apprehensively into the parking garage on Lower campus.

The walk from the parking garage to the gym proved even longer still, as I crept along as stealthily as possible, experiencing the uneasy feeling I so often feel in the face of adversity, slinking its way into the bowels of my stomach, making my apprehension ever-more intense. My legs were lead pipes and my feet concrete blocks as I waded through the quicksand that had replaced the sidewalks of Boston College since I left for summer vacation only two months prior. The gray, brick behemoth of a building, 21 Campanella Way, standing menacingly on my right, proved a formidable opponent, casting a shadow over me, stripping me of the sun as if the sun's light was my last lifeline to humanity – or perhaps to the old me – the me who hadn't received a phone call from Tyrese Rice. I slithered along; the shadow over my being, establishing itself as the true adversary here, bellowed of rocky waters ahead, as if it were a Siren and I were Odysseus. My head pulsed with a freshly erupting headache, my tongue and throat were the deserts of the Middle East, my saliva their once plush-green, fertile lands long-since dissolved by years of the most intense heat of the sun. My heart palpitated, numbing my extremities, quickening my pulse as if somehow my furtive prowl had become the all-out sprint of an Olympic gold medalist. I felt like a balloon in a sword shop; fragile, brittle, weak. I was a sinking ship, sending up my last signal flare in a no-way-out S.O.S. to end all S.O.S.'s.

Yet, to my own astonishment, I reached the hallowed doors of the Boston College Athletic Complex without the total catastrophic meltdown which had, at one point, felt so utterly imminent. The Titanic I had become had eluded each iceberg in my course and I had safely reached the serene harbors of New York. The discouragingly awesome darkness had retreated back to whatever corner of campus it had sprung from, and the sun actually began to shine (I suppose this is a cliché-like ending to the extended metaphor that was my walk from my car to the gym, but cliché or not, the sun was shining, and metaphor or not, that was one hell of a walk!). Power Gym was only a short elevator ride away, and I began to feel a slight tailwind in my sails that might just put me on cruise control as a bit of my apprehension released itself from my body. As I pulled open the doors, I experienced a complete cessation of worry as an avalanche of confidence spilled and thrust its way into my mind. I made my way to the elevator confident, poised, and ready for what I was about to face.

52 • College B

names like D
chills up a
perfect
for t
H

Chapter XI

The First Game of

"It was a high counsel that I once heard given to a young person,
– 'Always do what you are afraid to do.'"

- Ralph Waldo Emerson

It's ironic how things seem to work sometimes. I can remember both my drive from home to BC and my walk from my car to the gym in seemingly 21st-century, 1080p high-definition quality, however, what happened after I broke the threshold of Power Gymnasium lingers feebly in my memory in picture quality more like that of a nine inch, 1950s, black-and-white antenna television in a lightening storm – well, most of the finer details, anyway. I suppose I attribute this not so much to my failing memory, but rather, to the smokescreen thrown up by nerves I had thought I had under control. If my time with Boston College Basketball has taught me nothing else, it taught me that I ride a nerves roller coaster comparable to any thrill-ride on the planet.

When I walked into the gym, the guys had already begun the first game. I quickly laced up my Reebok ATR Pumps and got a quick stretch. (As I already mentioned, I could have the tightest muscles in the world. If I don't get a thorough stretch before I do anything athletically, there is an almost certainty that I'll pull a muscle. If I jump on the bed, I could pull a muscle. If I walk down the street, I could pull a muscle. If I played basketball without stretching, I would probably pull every muscle.) As I stretched, I caught myself gazing around the gym, just in awe at the sight of it, trying to take it all in, like a little kid who stands in front of a candy vending machine with a $10 bill. The first thing that caught my eye was the wall running perpendicular to the door I entered through. Displayed proudly along the top of the wall were all the names of the schools that participate in the Atlantic Coast Conference. Seeing

uke, North Carolina, Wake Forest, and Maryland sent
nd down my back without much effort at all. The floor was
- freshly redone (or, by the looks of this place, maybe just done
he first time) - so my feet almost stuck to it with each stride.
owever, if the huge gym, ACC banners, and brand new floor weren't
hint enough, I suppose it was the smell of the gym that told me "I
wasn't in Kansas anymore." It didn't smell like a high school gym at all,
or even a YMCA gym, rather, like it was too nice to be a gym - like I
didn't want to sweat in there, so as to not tarnish that smell. That smell
just seemed to make my nerves flare up, making me oddly apprehensive.
Sometimes I'm able to recapture that smell, just for fleeting instances,
and somehow, it still makes me nervous like it did that first time - like
it did every single time.

After my stretch, I noticed one of the guys not playing (he was the
11th man), and I decided to go introduce myself and shoot with him. It
turned out his name was Cortney Dunn, from Dallas, Texas, and my
initial reaction to him was that he was an outgoing and genuinely kind
person. As we shot, he talked a lot to me, which was truthfully more
than I expected from these hot-shot, big recruits. I remember one thing
Cortney told me that first day with vivid clarity. He said, "When you get
out there, just play basketball. Play as if you're not playing at BC, but
just like you're playing pick-up at the Y." This strangely sage advice from
my future freshman teammate caught me off-guard. He was exactly
right, though I didn't expect to hear such wise words from a complete
stranger. Nonetheless, I suppose this was the best advice I could have
heard at the time, seeing as how my nerves had once again become
wound tighter than the strings on a guitar.

Meanwhile, the game on the court had just ended - in an
argument, as most of our pick-up games would come to end throughout
the season - and Cortney and I replaced two of the other guys on the
losing team, ready to begin the next game. As each of them noticed me
come onto the court, their facial expressions began to change. Their
eyes were like stones; their looks were daggers being thrown in my
direction. Expressions of surprise and disbelief lined their faces, their
soundless mouths producing would-be words like, *Why is he playing?* and
Get out of here! While sometimes these awkward, wordless moments

prove to be the most difficult to handle as they weigh down on you with the weight of a thousand worlds, I suppose in that moment, I could be grateful that no one actually told me I couldn't play.

The game began and it went much the way I thought it would – a lot of being wide open and not much touching the ball. I knew respect was something that had to be earned, so I wasn't surprised at all when my first touch of the ball didn't come until the seventh or eighth possession of the game. Needless to say, I made the most of my first touch. I caught the ball on the right wing, only the result of a desperation pass – the result of an ill-advised picked up dribble – from the point guard, who I later learned was Biko Paris, from New Orleans, Louisiana. Without much hesitation, I swung the ball through to a triple threat position (this is a stance most basketball coaches teach their teams somewhere around the third grade level in which the player swings the ball to the "holster" of his hip on his shooting hand side, ready to either drive the ball to the hoop, shoot it, or pass it to a teammate), stepped across my body with my right foot (my first step has always been my most dangerous weapon), and took two hard, left-handed dribbles toward the hoop, culminating in a floater of deadly accuracy which swished through the net. (The floater is a move I had never attempted once in my career until this point, but with 7' shot blockers surrounding the basket like the moat around a castle, any guard could quickly learn the value of this simple move.) The rest of the game I didn't take a single shot – at least not one I can remember – and I don't remember who won the game.

I laugh whenever I think about this first day – for a few reasons. First, I have played a million pick-up games in my life, which means I have probably scored somewhere near five million pick-up game baskets, and I can remember very few of them with much clarity at all. However, this one seems as crystal clear in my mind as anything I've ever done. Second, it must have been a riot watching me play in that game. What I would have given to be a fly on that gym wall! When I play pick-up, I can always spot the scrub (and scrub here is no knock on anyone's personal hygiene, rather, just an expression basketball players give to the guy on the floor who really doesn't belong), and in this particular game, for the first time in my career, I was certainly the scrub. I must have looked like a bull in a china shop, running and jumping with limited coordination, at least when compared to the guys I was running and jumping with. Finally, and most importantly, the basket about which I just wrote nearly a page mattered almost as much as a misplaced raven in a convocation of eagles.

Think about that for a second or two. What would a group of majestic eagles think when soaring next to a mangy raven? Perhaps, *Why is he soaring with us?* or *He isn't big enough!* or *He isn't fast enough!* or *Is he for real?* But for the raven...Oh, for the raven! What a thrill it must be for him to fly with the Eagles! What must the raven think?

Chapter XII

Al Skinner's Summer School of Basketball

"It's a sad funny ending to find yourself pretending,
a *poor* man in a *rich* man's shirt."

- Bruce Springsteen (with apologies), "Better Days"

The rest of the summer continued in much the same fashion. I routinely made the trip up to Boston College, and contrary to popular belief, each trip proved equally as difficult as the time before. Sometimes I would make the hour-long drive, my nerves and adrenaline building ferociously the entire way, only to arrive and find out that the gym was closed and we weren't playing that day. Sometimes I would arrive and the rest of the guys would be leaving the gym, just having finished their run for the day. One time, I even walked into the complex toward the elevator and was stopped by a BC Athletics employee. I told him I was here to play pick-up with the basketball team, and his God-honest response was, "Sure, and I'm the Pope." He "escorted" me from the premises and subsequently, stood guard of the door for the next 10 minutes.

Now, you may be thinking, *Why didn't you just call someone?* or *Why couldn't you talk to someone to let you in?* or any other number of obvious questions. The truth is, however, that there was no one I could call and no one I could talk to. I had Tyrese's number and even left him a message once, just pleading for him to call me if they weren't playing or if the game time changed, but he never returned the call. I didn't know anyone else on the team at this point, especially not well enough to have him call me. Furthermore, who would I turn to outside the team? Coach Skinner? He'd never said a word to me. Doug Flutie? I think you get my point... It was sadly just one of those terrible situations where all you can do is smile and roll with the punches, even if it seemed to be Mike Tyson throwing them.

As the weeks of the summer slunk by with "stuck-in-the-mud" slow-footedness, my anticipation for October 15, 2007 (the first day of sanctioned NCAA practice) grew more and more intense, despite the number of disappointing miles I had put on my car over the course of recent weeks and the number of times I had made the trip only to make an immediate about-face.

As July neared its end, I received a call from Director of Basketball Operations Preston Murphy asking me if I wanted to work Coach Skinner's Summer School of Basketball camp. I probably should have realized that this invitation was a sign that they were simply short-staffed; however, I took it as a chance to spend some time with my new teammates and get to know them a little better, and if nothing else, at least I'd be able to get some shots up at Power Gym after camp each day.

On the first day of camp, I had an interesting dilemma on my hands: Do I leave Northbridge at 7:00 a.m. to arrive in Newton at 8:45 a.m. (taking into account early-morning commute Massachusetts Turnpike traffic), with camp starting promptly at 9:00 a.m., or do I leave closer to 6:00 a.m., beat traffic, and arrive in Newton two hours early at 7:00 a.m.? Not wanting to be late on the first day of camp, I elected the latter, arriving as expected, almost two hours early. When I parked my car in the parking garage, I reclined my seat and took a nap until 8:30, when I went into camp.

When I got up to Power Gym (where camp was being held), I bumped into John Oates, whom I hadn't yet met because he hadn't been playing pick-up due to a foot injury he was nursing. After the typical introductions, he asked me if I'd seen the locker room yet, and unknowingly, I said, "No, but a locker room is a locker room, right?" He smirked and told me to follow him. He led me out of Power, down a short carpeted corridor, and punched in a code on a door that read "Boston College Men's Basketball: Locker Room." Nothing I had ever seen, and certainly no locker room I'd ever been in, could prepare me for what I was about to see.

As he opened the door, the smell of that horrid place literally attacked me, leaping from the bowels of the room, smothering me in a rank, molded mildew cloud from which I couldn't escape. As we proceeded cautiously down the poorly lit, 19th-century staircase toward the main chamber of the place, the smell became seemingly alive, reaching out with its shapeless clutches and disorienting my senses.

The one hanging light flickered off and on, its thin, inverted halo of luminance failing to offer us much comfort as the wooden stairs creaked and whined under each step we took, threatening to give way with each shrill cry. I tried to keep my eyes on the wall of off-yellow light emanating from the door-less entryway at the stairs' landing, trying to convince myself that if I made it down the stairs, everything would be okay. However, halfway down the descent into what was resembling the Inferno more and more with each step, I spotted the shadowed, dust-blanketed outline of something carved into the concrete of the wall. As I wiped the dust covering away with my forearm, my blood froze in my veins and goose bumps leapt from my skin as the message was unveiled: ABANDON EVERY HOPE, ALL YOU WHO ENTER. I begged John to turn around, but he urged me to forge ahead.

As we reached the bottom of the stairs, the smell became even more severe, burning my nose, while the yellowed wall of light became the orange and brown water marks staining every inch of the walls. Fallen ceiling panels and sinking water pipes formed the roof to this room and old, cracking cement was the floor. Splintered wooden benches stood erect in front of two walls of decrepit lockers, only about half had properly working doors. Puddles of drip-water from overhead pipes polka-dotted the floor, creating land mines of shoe-soaking disaster, which I tried to avoid at all costs.

Down the hall from the mildewed main chamber hid a bathroom, complete with one working sink and a yellow toilet with an almost-broken flusher. A sour smell oozed from this cell of the dungeon and mingled with the mold smell of the main chamber, creating an aroma cocktail like nothing I had ever smelled. All I could do was turn to John and ask him why he brought me to this place. However, when I turned to him fire erupted from his eyes and horns shot out of his skull, his sinister laugh filling the room like the reverberating sounds from a Hell organ playing all the wrong notes... Okay, okay, so I guess I'll stop that story right here. That was obviously not the locker room at Boston College, and John Oates obviously didn't turn into some organ-playing fire demon. However, that description of the locker room was, more or less, how my high school football locker room was, and I only add this story as a light-hearted contrast to the true BC Basketball locker room!

As he opened the real locker room door, the first thing I noticed was the hardwood floor. The gold-outlined words "Boston College" lined the polished wood of the narrow strip of corridor leading to the two main rooms of the locker room (yes, the *two* main rooms). At the end of the short strip, carpet replaced the hardwood as I entered the first of the two rooms on the left side of the fork. As I entered this room, I was almost shocked at what I saw. A 60-inch LCD HD TV stood triumphantly at the front-center of the room, surrounded by a company of black leather sofas and armchairs. Hiding on one of the shelves of the TV stand under the television was a Playstation 3, equipped with a whole horde of games. To the left of the mammoth TV was a refrigerator and to its left, a large audio deck from which the volume of the sound system running throughout the locker room along the tops of the walls was controlled. The walls of the TV room (as I'll refer to it) were lined with pictures of BC Basketball heroes past and present. Players like Troy Bell, Jared Dudley, Tyrese Rice, and John Oates cast a constant reminder to the players sitting in that room of the years of success and greatness of the Boston College Basketball program. Painted on the wall nearest to the entrance to the TV room was a giant mural of a great eagle exploding out from Conte Forum, soaring over the mascots of the other 11 ACC teams. Finally, along the far wall, blazoned above the television, were the eight-inch tall, embossed maroon words "EVER TO EXCEL," which I came to know as the Boston College Athletics motto. (It might have been altogether more appropriate had that blazoned motto read "SEE ONCE MORE THE STARS." Perhaps it would have had Dante designed the room.)

After picking my jaw up off the floor, I moved to the right into the other main room of the locker room, this room actually being the room with the lockers. As I walked into this room, I noticed that carpet still lined the floor, much unlike the concrete or tiled floors of all the locker rooms I'd ever been in. Each player's locker was a 7'-high, double-door, wooden combination locker, each complete with the player's name and number displayed proudly at its summit, as well as on the wall above the locker, however, this time, accompanied by an action-shot game photo. In front of each locker sat a leather-topped stool as well. On the far end of this room, I could see a bathroom and shower room, too, and walking through the bathroom, one could loop back around to the first main room (as the rooms formed a continuous path) or one could continue through a large wooden door to the coaches' offices. At this point, all I could do was chuckle. This was the locker room. This was *my* locker room.

****

After channeling my inner Magellan and circumnavigating the locker room a few times, I made my way out toward the bleachers of Conte Forum, where the camp counselors were meeting before camp began. I can't even describe the flood of emotion that washed over me when I walked into Conte Forum and saw the arena for the first time. I had been in Conte Forum plenty of times, but each time it was jam-packed with people, all watching a basketball or hockey game. To see it on this day – empty and *new* – made me feel like Columbus landing in the New World (to continue with my 15th/16th century explorer metaphor). I just wanted to run down onto the floor, like a kid on Christmas morning, and shoot until I couldn't stand anymore. The worst part of it was that I had to pretend like it was all commonplace to me; I had to act like it didn't faze me to be here.

For me, seeing Conte Forum – really seeing it for the first time – was like walking up from the main concourse, through the tunnels, to field level at Fenway Park. You see the top of the Monster creeping into view, followed by the scoreboard, and finally, the greenest grass the world has to offer catches your eye as you see the field for the first time. For me, at that moment, as the goosebumps and butterflies wage war to see who takes over, there is just no way not to smile. And even though I've been to Fenway more than 25 times, each time is just as special for me. I couldn't imagine anyone not being in awe at that sight. To some extent, the same held true at Conte Forum on the first day of camp. I couldn't believe my eyes when I saw people who weren't just swallowed up by the atmosphere of the place. The 8,606 seats surrounding the court like a maroon blanket, the freshly lacquered hardwood emblazoned with gold lettering, reading "Boston College Eagles," and the countless championship banners hanging from the rafters made the place seem so picturesque. At that moment, I was even more excited for the start of the season than I had ever been before. Somehow, however, I found a way to hide my excitement behind a seemingly jaded mask and pretended I wasn't literally bursting at the seams with jubilance.

After we had received our instructions, we made our way into Power Gym, where the campers, ranging in age from eight to 13, were shooting hoops and anxiously awaiting our arrival. I suppose the word "our" here isn't quite the right word; perhaps "Tyrese, Daye, John, Shamari, and Tyrelle's" arrivals would have been the more appropriate phrase choice for this situation. After all, at this point, I hadn't had a try-out yet, wasn't officially on the roster, and wasn't even allowed to work out with the team in the weight room. In fact, the only Boston College Basketball attire I even owned was the complementary shirt all of the camp coaches got at the beginning of the first day. And truth be told, of all of the BC Basketball guys working the camp this week, I am pretty certain that only Tyrese and maybe John even knew my name. So, to say the kids were not quite anxiously awaiting my arrival is probably a bit of an understatement.

As the days of that week passed, I found myself in a bit of a rhythm. I would leave my house at 6:00 a.m., arrive at BC around 7:00 a.m., head up to the locker room, and take an hour-long nap on one of the black leather sofas. I would set an alarm on my cell phone to wake me up around 8:15, when the first of the other coaches would come rolling in, to avoid the awkward "Why are you sleeping in the locker room?" question. Camp would begin at 9:00 a.m. and my team would proceed to lose every game the entire week, obviously putting me in last place, which at a kids' basketball camp, means almost nothing, except to the coaches, who use their place in the standings as bragging rights and as obvious proof as to who is the best coach and player among them. However, since I already knew I was the worst player among them, and knew that I'd probably receive no respect from the kids because I wasn't

Tyrese, I wasn't overly shocked or dismayed at the performance of my team, which ironically was named N.C. State, who finished near the bottom in the ACC in the 2006-2007 season.

One thing about camp that particularly bothered me, however, was the trivia game at the end of each day. Coach Mo Cassara, one of the assistant coaches at BC, and the coach who was running the camp, would stand up in front of the camp and ask the kids trivia questions about the current BC Eagles players – questions like "Where did Tyrese Rice go to high school?" or "What school is Joe Trapani transferring from?" Each day he'd ask a few questions about different players, and when the kids would answer them correctly, they'd get a prize. However, it wasn't the kids who were the most excited about their chance to win a prize; but rather, it was me who was most anxious about the trivia game because each day I hoped Coach Cassara would ask a question about me. In my mind, if he asked a question about me, it would solidify my spot on the roster as the walk-on and get the eight-ton gorilla off my back. However, to my dismay, the question never came and my unease about whether or not I'd be on the team remained, and if anything, grew more intense. Ultimately, I wouldn't know if I made the team until Wednesday, October 17th, two days after we began practice!

Chapter XIII

The First Day of Practice

"Our greatest glory is not in never falling
but in rising every time we fall."

- Confucius

Have you ever noticed that when you're going somewhere or doing something - let's say a vacation to Disney World - it always seems to take ages to get there, but only minutes to get home? The simple answer to this "phenomenon" is that there is a build-up of anticipation in your mind - anticipation to get to Disney World, in this case - and it is that longing to arrive, ride the rides, see the attractions, and give a great big hug to Mickey Mouse that makes it seem like it takes forever to get there. By definition, anticipation is an emotion, involving pleasure or anxiety, in considering some expected or longed-for event (or the irritation at having to wait for this event). Robert Plutchik, a 20th-century psychologist, listed anticipation as one of the eight basic emotions in his psychoevolutionary theory of emotion. However, I found it very puzzling that there were actually seven other emotions Plutchik classified, because in the six weeks from September 3rd when classes began for my sophomore year, until October 15th when practice officially began, anticipation was the only emotion I could feel. I was living, breathing, sleeping, and dreaming anticipation for the beginning of basketball. It seemed like every other emotion I could have - hunger, want, tiredness, anger, and even love - were replaced by just this longing to get this basketball snowball rolling downhill.

The first six weeks of class seemed to drag their feet, taking what seemed like six years to scuffle away. It almost seemed like some diabolical little kid had crept up on the hourglass of time, unscrewed the top, and added just a few drops of water to the sand - just enough to clog the hole the sand falls through, slowing down time to a grinding, screeching, whining halt. However, after what seemed like a billion lifetimes, October 15th, 2007 finally arrived, like the first warm, golden rays of spring after a long, bleak, colorless winter. (T.S. Eliot wrote in his masterpiece, *The Waste Land*, that "April is the cruelest month," – for his own reasons – however, I am here to argue that point. The first six weeks of the school year, leading up to the start of basketball practices, are undoubtedly the cruelest!)

On the first day of practice, I arrived at the BC Athletics complex considerably early, about 1:00 p.m. for a 2:00 p.m. practice. Our practices typically ran from 2:00-4:00; sometimes we'd only go until 3:45, while other times we'd practice right until 4:30 when the women's team took over the gym.

When I arrived in the locker room on the first day, I noticed everyone's locker was open, a practice uniform – jersey, shorts, and socks – hung neatly on a laundry belt (a belt-like device on which we would clip our practice gear or game uniforms after we finished practicing or playing in order to have our laundry done for us) inside the lockers. Each practice jersey and pair of shorts was reversible and displayed each player's number on the back of the shirt and leg of the shorts. I remember seeing those uniforms and feeling that feeling of unrestrained joy seeping out through the smile on my face. I felt like I was finally part of the team. I felt like it was finally official. I went over to my locker, the closest locker to the front of the room, near the white board where Coach Skinner would draw up the game plans, on the right side of the room, only to be utterly deflated as I discovered no glorious jersey occupying the hooks in my locker.

It occurred to me that there was no way the equipment manager could have known that this was my locker because, unlike everyone else's lockers which proudly displayed their names and an action-shot game picture of them, my locker was completely bare, simply saying "Boston College Basketball" at the top. There were three other lockers, in the back of the locker room, that weren't occupied, so I figured perhaps my long-awaited uniform was hanging in one of those. With this theory I was only fooling myself, however, my search ending with no avail; no uniform for me hung in any of the lockers.

Following my disappointment in the locker room, I decided to venture downstairs to the ground floor level of the complex (Power Gym and our locker room were on the second floor), and seek out the equipment manager to ask him for a practice uniform. When I finally tracked him down, I asked him for what I needed, and he told me he didn't have anything for me. He was not an overly friendly person to me, but he certainly never gave me even half the resistance some of the other BC Athletics personnel would throw my way in the following months. I told him that I needed something to practice in, and he told me he'd try to find something in the back, but he wouldn't promise anything. A few minutes later he emerged from the back of the equipment room with an unnumbered Reebok practice jersey and a pair of Reebok shorts (both XXL), a pair of Under Armour compression shorts, and a few pairs of Reebok socks. Almost everything we were given, in terms of athletic gear, was Reebok brand. Boston College is one of the few collegiate sports teams that Reebok does business with (most collegiate teams have other sponsors like Nike, Russell Athletic, etc., while Reebok sponsors a lot of professional sports teams). The fact that all of my equipment was XXL made things a bit awkward. I am the kind of basketball player who likes my uniform to be more on the snug side. I don't like my jersey hanging off me so people can grab and hold it, and I don't like my shorts hanging below my knees because it impedes the bend in my knee, slowing me down. However, in this situation, I had no choice, and I graciously took what I was given – even though the XXL was designed for someone standing about 6' 8", rather than my 6'.

At 2:00, practice began with great intensity, and we began the most up-tempo lay-up lines I'd ever been a part of. I had so much adrenaline pumping through me that I felt like I could touch the ceiling. However, what were flowing through me even more intensely than my adrenaline were my nerves. I was more nervous at this moment than in any other moment in my entire life. In a phrase, I was a train wreck waiting to happen. I finally reached the front of the right lay-up line, everything seeming to be getting fuzzy, my eyes seeing only in a strange tunnel-vision, everything blackening except for the ball and my path to the basket. I caught the ball, took three hard dribbles to the basket, jumped off my left foot, powering toward the basket, and lost the ball. I felt the basketball slip from my hands and clank miserably off the crevice between the bottom of the rim and backboard. I can only imagine what this must have looked like for the other guys on the team – something a bit less graceful than Bambi on ice. I remember the way the other guys began to laugh, hooting and hollering that I missed my lay-up. I felt like an actor on stage who had forgotten his lines, the white-hot spotlight bearing down on me, piercing my skin with a heat-of-the-sun intensity. Each jeering word and mocking laugh seemed to cut me deeper and deeper, my nerves swelling and crashing like giant waves crashing over the retaining wall of my sanity. The sweat poured from my body, a sickening testament to the gross nervousness coursing through my veins. It was so hard for me to be scoffed at like that. All I wanted was to be accepted and liked by my teammates. I didn't need them to think I was Michael Jordan; I simply wanted them to like me and respect me as an individual. Needless to say, that was starting off on the wrong foot.

I felt like giving up. I felt the familiar feeling of walking out of the gym and saying goodbye to basketball forever regaining its stranglehold on me. That voice in my head told me to stay, however. That voice that reminds me every day how much I love the game convinced me that this would be an obstacle I would have no problem surmounting if I just didn't give up.

The next time my turn came around in the lay-up line I made my lay-up without even thinking about it. I just caught the ball, dribbled hard, and laid the ball off the glass, like I had done countless millions of times in my life. I slowly began to regain that lost adrenaline and had begun to shake the tunnel vision that had consumed me earlier as well. I began to notice, however, that instead of laying the ball gently off the glass, most of the guys on the team, save one or two, were thunderously dunking the ball, taking no chances in meeting with a similar fate as my own. While I am only a generous 6' tall, I have occasionally dunked the ball in my day. The conditions have to be perfect for me though. I have to be in a gym, adrenaline flowing, and I have to be loose and limber. However, if all these conditions are met, I can sometimes get enough lift to slam a ball through. I figured all of these aforementioned conditions were met and I had as much adrenaline as I'd ever have, so when my turn came around again, I caught the ball, took two power dribbles, and jumped off of two feet, stretching the ball toward the rim in my left hand as far as I could reach. I felt myself soar toward the hoop, get the ball above the rim, and thrust it downward. However, like I have done more often than not, I threw the ball off the back of the rim before grabbing onto the front, the ball flying away in another missed attempt.

I couldn't believe it! My second missed lay-up of the day. I should have just laid the ball off the glass and softly erased my first miss. But I had to try to show off to the team and coaches and missed another shot. I remember hearing two things very distinctly after I missed the dunk. First, I heard Coach yell, "If you can't dunk, lay it in!" something he would yell quite frequently throughout the year, typically in mockery of one of our high-flyers, however, only that once would he have to yell it at me. The second thing I heard was what really scared me. All of the older guys on the team were hissing, "Feezy! Feezy!" At this point, I had no idea what a feezy was, and to my chagrin, I would soon learn what it means the hard way. When I skulked back to the end of the rebounding line, Preston Murphy, the Director of Basketball Operations and the guy I had played pick-up with every day the previous semester, asked me if I knew I had to run if I missed lay-ups. "How in God's name could I possibly know I had to run if I missed lay-ups?!" I felt like shouting, but all I managed to squeak out was, "No."

After the lay-up lines, Coach Skinner yelled, "Line 'em up!" (I suppose here is a good time to make it known that when I say Coach Skinner "yelled," I really mean that he said it in more than just a soft voice. Coach Skinner is a very soft-spoken person and very rarely yells. However, he doesn't have to yell often because his presence commands a great deal of respect from his players, so when he speaks, we all listen.) Having missed two lay-ups, and in fact being the only one who missed any lay-ups, I lined up on the baseline, ready to do my running. It would be the loneliest run of my career, having to run a sprint by myself in front of my new teammates, most of them still not knowing my name. As Coach prepared to yell, "Let's go!," (he never blew a whistle, rather, just yelled) I was surprised to see that Tyrelle Blair, our center from Monticello, Florida, had stepped up to the baseline to join me in the sprint. I, to this day, cannot thank Tyrelle enough for that act. It showed his outstanding character, as well as his kindness – two things that truly are a rarity in today's world. On top of that, it was a good thing he stepped up because I had no idea what kind of sprint I was running. A down and back? A suicide? I had no clue. When Coach yelled to begin, I just followed Tyrelle's lead. It clearly wasn't a suicide, as we ran completely down the court to the other baseline, so I figured it was a down and back. However, when we reached the original baseline, we turned and began to run again. I figured it was just two down and backs then, because I had missed two lay-ups. However, when we returned to the starting line, we simply turned back and kept running. It turns out that a feezy is actually called a "full-court five," which means we have to complete five full-court sprints (down and backs), a total of 10 sprints, in one minute. I remember running those in high school on occasion (we called them "10s"), but in high school they were neither timed nor a punishment for missing two lay-ups. In high school, they were reserved for when we truly messed up beyond reason and Coach Baker, my high school coach, wanted to make it known that we were never to do whatever it was we had done again.

Following my first feezy, I felt like my legs were completely shot – like someone had cruelly replaced my bones with titanium and my muscles with...more titanium. I felt like there were knives in my lungs – like every inhalation of the gym's cold air was another dagger slashing a hole in my insides, preventing me from catching my breath. My heart was beating like a drum (not some little bongo drums, but more like one of those gigantic bass drums in the parades), bouncing off the walls of my rib cage in a frantic attempt to leap from my chest and catch the next train out of Boston. My knees felt wobbly, as if I would collapse if my mind didn't totally focus all my effort on remaining upright. This feeling of exhaustion was amplified tenfold, however, because I was trying to make a great impression on my coaches. I feel like whenever I have *that* much adrenaline pumping and the stage is *that* magnificent, my energy level always seems to deplete rather quickly.

I remember every time I'd gone somewhere to "try-out" or show a coach "what I can do" in the past – The University of Rochester and Wesleyan University – my legs seemed to fail me far too quickly in the showcase. Perhaps it is the fact that I am trying so desperately to make a good impression that I literally gas myself by going a hundred miles per hour the entire time. Perhaps it is just the simple fact that I am not as well conditioned as some of these athletes. Either way, the same held very true - possibly more so - for my first Boston College practice. Literally, by 2:20 p.m., I felt as though I could have dug a hole in the middle of the practice floor, swan dived into it, and died. Ironically, I remember telling my father on the phone before my first practice that I wanted to try to conserve energy to the best of my ability. I suppose I probably should have knocked on wood or something after that comment!

If I was asked to break down my own game and find weaknesses and flaws in it, I would have to label conditioning as the one area of my game that has always held me back (if I had to place the label of "weakness" somewhere). I guess it hasn't really ever truly impeded my success in basketball; however, what I'm trying to say is that it just takes me quite some time to really get into "game shape." While some players can step out onto the court on the first day of practice and just run for two hours straight, others, like me, require a few weeks of serious conditioning to achieve top conditioning.

I remember thinking for the rest of that first practice that I just wanted to fade away, slink along the wall, and sneak unnoticed out the gym's back door and never come back. (I think it's important to note here that I never really have any intention of giving up - ever. It's just a natural thought to want to quit when you feel like your lungs are going to collapse and your heart is about to burst in your chest.)

After lay-up lines, Coach Skinner put in our first play - flex - which was to be the staple of our offense. Flex is a very methodical offense. It requires tight, sharp cuts and a closely packed spacing scheme. The goal of flex is to drain the shot clock, make the defense defend for 30 seconds, and then to get a back door cut or elbow jumper when the defense lets up for a split second.

I have heard quite a few people criticize Coach Skinner for running this type of offense in the ACC. Most people say it worked great in the Big East (the conference that BC used to be in prior to 2003) or that it worked well with players like Craig Smith and Jared

Dudley, but that it couldn't work with the current roster. For me, however, I didn't really care what the critics had to say because flex was the offense I ran in high school, so I knew it well. While it isn't the most difficult offense to learn, it was just one less thing for me to worry about, and therefore, a moment's relief. Coach Skinner didn't actually call his offense "flex" however, because often in ACC play, the arenas get too loud to hear play calls, so we were instructed to use hand signals to call out our plays. Flex soon became known as "chop," and was designated by a chopping motion of the point guard's hand. We also put in a play called "side chop," obviously designated by the point guard chopping his hand in a sideways motion. This simply told the other four players that the point guard was going to enter the ball to a different spot and the play just threw in a simple wrinkle at the beginning of the motion, which I easily picked up.

Later, we broke up into "guards and bigs," to do a bit of drilling. We did most of the standard first practice drills – two-ball dribbling, shooting off of picks, defending screens, guard-guard switches on defense, etc. However, as we did each drill, I just felt a bit slow – a step or two "behind" everyone else. It's just very difficult for me – 6', 185 pounds – to guard a person "straight up" who is quicker than me and stands 6' 5" and weighs 225 pounds. Quite literally, the physics are not in my favor.

Practice continued with mostly conditioning drills, as most first practices do. We did a few more feezies, a few foot-fire drills, some lane slides, and finished up with a full-court conditioning drill which we called "backboard taps" in high school, but only did this one time at BC. For backboard taps, we formed two lines, one at each foul line on the court. The first person in line would throw the basketball off the backboard and the next person in line would have to run up, catch the ball while jumping, and throw it off the backboard for the next person. After the person threw the ball off the backboard, he would have to sprint the length of the floor and repeat the same process on the other end of the court. Now, in high school, this was one of the most difficult conditioning drills we could do. We would do it for one minute and often, we'd fumble the ball or throw it over the backboard and we'd have to start over. I understand that a minute is not that long of a time

- only 60 seconds - however, when you're doing a drill like this, one minute can seem like one hour. And unlike high school, at Boston College, we did this drill for three minutes! Needless to say, I was literally running on fumes at this point. If my first feezy wasn't enough to wear me out, the other feezies, lane slides, and foot fires were certainly enough to do the trick.

Another aspect of BC practice that is worth noting is the fact that many practices we'd only get one water break, and at BC, water breaks were one-minute, timed breaks. If anyone took a drink after the buzzer sounded, we'd have to run a feezy, which would ultimately negate the water break. However, giving up was not a choice at this point in my first practice, and I reluctantly made my way to the free throw line, taking a few deep breaths before the drill began.

I remember the three minutes on that clock seemed to tick away about as casually as possible. At one point, I am pretty certain the clock actually froze for a good 10 seconds or so. At about the two-minute mark, I felt like even the fumes I had been previously running on were exhausted and my engine was about to seize up entirely. The seconds slowly melted away - melting like a snowman melts on a 50-degrees-below-zero January day in the North Pole. In the last 15 seconds, one of my teammates began to fade and I had to pass him to keep the ball off the ground. This pass took every ounce of energy I had left in my body, but it was well worth it because we didn't have to run for another three minutes. When the buzzer sounded and that drill ended, I was the most tired I had ever been in my entire life - something that remains the case to this day. It was like someone replaced my spine with an L-shaped pole because I couldn't get my hands off my knees to stand up straight. I felt like I would never catch my breath again. However, the good news was that many of my teammates were in the same boat as me - many of them hunched over, gasping for air as well. Taking some positive out of that first practice, I learned that I wasn't quite in as poor shape, conditioning-wise, as I thought entering the practice, which gave me some small peace of mind in the upcoming weeks. I can honestly say, though, that I have never been so relieved to hear a coach say, "Bring it in," in my entire career. After practice, I gumshoed out of the gym, limping into the locker room, hoping no one would give me grief about my feezy or my lack of conditioning. I quickly (and quickly is a subjective term here because for me, "quickly" after practice actually means "sluggishly") strung my practice jersey and shorts on my laundry loop and made my way back to my dorm, where I instantly collapsed into my bed and fell asleep until the next morning. While I could hardly fathom the thought of practice the next day, I knew it would come and I knew I'd somehow be ready for it.

Chapter XIV
It's "Official" – Or is it?

"The greatest mistake you can make in life is to
be continually fearing you will make one."

- Elbert Hubbard, *The Note Book of Elbert Hubbard*

Two days after practice started – or what I was still apprehensively calling my try-out, despite Murph's assurance that there would be no official try-out – I received notification that my place on the team was finally "official." I had been sitting in Molecular Biology class when my phone began to ring. When I picked it up I learned that it was my buddy, Andy Paolino, from my intramural team, and the first thing he said was, "Congratulations man!"

Naturally, my reaction was, "For what?"

"For making the damn team, moron!"

To be completely honest, I had no clue why he was saying this. I thought maybe he missed something and was just congratulating me like most others had for "making the team," when in reality, I was still (at least in my mind) trying-out.

"Well they haven't told me anything for sure yet, but the practices are going okay," I told him.

"I guess you haven't checked the website then. Check out the roster!"

In fact, I hadn't checked the basketball website in quite some time. Instantly, I whipped open my computer, typed in the URL for the BC Athletics homepage, selected basketball, and clicked on the roster. I couldn't believe my eyes! There I was, three spots from the top, and I had been assigned number 10:

No.	Name	Cl.	Pos.	Ht.	Wt.	High School/ Hometown
10	Brennan Bennett	SO	Guard	6-0	185	Northbridge / Whitinsville, MA

It was like catching a glimpse of Heaven. I felt like I was floating, flying, soaring, walking on air, or any other of the million cheesy taglines expressing the incredible euphoria I was experiencing at that moment. My hands were shaking and my extremities became tingly. Needless to say, I wasn't really in the mood for biology anymore, so I packed up my things and sneaked out the back of the classroom, immediately calling my parents to tell them the great news. However, while I told everyone about the validity of my roster spot, I still held quite a bit of trepidation regarding the "concrete nature" of this position. By this, I simply mean that I held a bit of doubt that my making the official roster meant I was on the team for sure. I still felt like I could be cut at any moment and I didn't want to get my hopes up that anything was for certain. After all, how easily could the website moderator just delete my name from the roster? It would probably take less time to delete me than it took to add me, and just like that, my five minutes of fame would be over.

My consternation was undoubtedly a direct result of a story I had heard from some of the guys on the team throughout the first few days of practice. Each practice, we do a free throw shooting drill in which we have to make 40 out of 50 free throws as a team or we have to run a feezy. Apparently, at the onset of the 2006-2007 season, a kid tried out as a walk-on (with one other kid who was instantly cut upon walking in the gym because he was wearing University of North Carolina shorts to a BC try-out), made the team, had his name added to the roster, received practice gear, got his locker and combination, and a few days later, was informed that he had been cut because he couldn't make a free throw and he was making the team run every day. For at least a week after I discovered my name on the roster I was extremely wary of the possibility that missing a free throw could place my head on the proverbial chopping block.

Probably the tidbit of information that made me the most nervous was something that John Oates told me. I remember him telling me that when this walk-on would miss a bunch of free throws, it wasn't the coaches who would get upset, but rather, it was the other players who clamored for his release from the team. This fact - the fact that if enough players made enough noise about any flaws I had in my game - scared me the most; it meant that I could meet with the same misfortune as the aforementioned walk-on if enough guys complained about me. I decided that I would consider nothing totally official until I was holding a Boston College number 10 uniform in my hands with BENNETT hemmed across the back. Ironically, I would be holding my number 10 jersey in only a few short days; however, it did nothing to ease my troubled mind.

Chapter XV

The Team Poster

"Little minds are tamed and subdued by misfortunes;
but great minds rise above them."

- Washington Irving, *The Sketch Book of Geoffrey Crayon*

After two weeks of practice, my spot on the team was still intact. I had played relatively well in practice, not turning the ball over much and making the majority of my free throws. While I certainly didn't stand out among the rest of the players on the team, I definitely gave no one any reason to call for my head. With each passing day, I became more and more confident in my place in the program and the rope restraining the free fall of the guillotine blade became more and more secure.

One day before practice, we were called into the locker room for a team meeting. We were having a meeting with a representative from Reebok who was going to supply us with some team shoes and some other Reebok gear for the season. Now, allow me to make it very clear that I have never been on a team that has been *supplied* with anything. In high school, we "got team shoes" my junior year, but in reality, each player just went to Foot Locker or Dick's Sporting Goods and paid $125 for the LeBrons, and if memory serves me correctly, only about nine of the 14 guys on the varsity team even bought the "team shoes." My senior year we "got team sweat suits," each one costing us nearly $100, and mine was actually my Christmas present from my parents. Even in middle school basketball we "got team sweatshirts," but again, each player was responsible for paying the $35 for the gear, or $45 if we wanted our name and number embroidered on the sleeve. I only highlight these few examples because I want to emphasize the complete and utter astonishment that consumed every fiber of my being when I learned that as a member of the BC Basketball program, I would be receiving seven pairs of Reebok basketball shoes (one white home pair, one black and maroon away pair, one gold pair for Saturday games, and four others for the nationally-televised games), four different Reebok Boston College Basketball sweat suits (two specifically for travel), and countless Reebok BC shooting shirts, both long-sleeve and short-sleeve! The most incredible part of this, however, was the simple fact that all this *stuff* cost me my favorite price of all – "*free* ninety-nine!"

On top the mountain of Reebok gear we were to receive, we were also given a travel suitcase with our number embroidered on it a few times, a travel gym bag, as many pairs of Reebok socks as we would need in 10 lifetimes, free Under-Armour compression shorts, and even a Boston College winter hat.

*****

We were told after practice one day that we would be taking pictures for the team poster in two days and we were to come prepared. In the midst of all the excitement and trepidation of the first few weeks of practice, I had completely forgotten that each year BC Basketball, Football, Hockey, and Baseball put out a team poster displaying each member of the team dressed in full uniform. In my mind, if this poster was produced with me proudly wearing my uniform as a part of it, my spot on the team would be officially, once-and-for-all, without a shadow of a doubt, solidified, so needless to say, I was rather excited for the next day's proceedings.

The next day when I entered the locker room before practice, I was ecstatic to find a pair of white and maroon Reebok basketball shoes in my locker. However, upon looking around, I discovered that each of the other members of the team had received three pairs of shoes; they had received the same standard white Reeboks, but also the same pair in black and maroon and another pair of gold shoes, too. I immediately went down to the equipment manager to inquire about the reason for my not receiving the other two pairs of shoes, and upon my inquisition, I was informed that the equipment manager didn't have the other two pairs for me because he didn't have them in a size 12. This struck me as odd, simply because if he had ordered them through the Reebok representative with whom we had spoken only the day before, why would he have ordered me a pair of white Reeboks in size 12, but not the other two pairs of shoes in size 12? It would actually be another week and a half before I would receive the other two pairs of shoes, actually getting them just days before the first game against New Hampshire.

*****

The following day, when I entered the locker room for the team poster pictures, I noticed that everyone's gold uniforms – shorts and shirts – were hanging in their lockers. However, when I came to my locker, I noticed that it was vacant. (One could only imagine my thought process in that moment. If my reader hasn't already noticed, I'm a bit of a worrisome person. I like to have things planned out, or in this case, I like when things work themselves out smoothly or when things just go the way they're *supposed* to go. My life would have been so much easier had my jersey just been in my locker that day. However, as I briefly touched on earlier in this piece, things rarely, if ever, turn out the way we intend them to.)

Finding my locker completely empty, and noticing that many of my teammates were already clad in their gold uniforms, I decided to run down to the equipment manager and find out why my jersey was conspicuously absent from its place in my locker. (I want my reader to pay particular attention to the use of the word "completely" in the first sentence of this paragraph. I say *completely* empty because each night the equipment manager comes into the locker room to get the laundry to bring downstairs to the laundry room to have washed for the next day, and on the night before, my laundry was actually in my locker because I forgot to throw it in the laundry container. Because my locker was locked, the equipment manager had to use a key to open it to get my laundry. However, when he got my practice gear out, he forgot to relock my locker and the next day, before we took poster pictures, I not only neglected to find my gold uniform, but I also noticed that the two Reebok shooting shirts I had hanging in my locker were also missing. Someone had actually stolen my shirts – and hangers – out of my locker, and not surprisingly, I never discovered who the culprit was. I quickly realized that in this locker room, "what was mine was yours, and what was yours, was only yours.")

When I got down to the equipment manager's office, I found him in the equipment room in the back. When I asked him about my jersey, he said, "I don't have one for you." I felt like yelling, *"What do you mean you don't have one for me!? How can you just not have one for me!? Am I not on the team!? Am I not a jersey-wearing, uniform-toting member of this team!?"* It was one of those moments when you're just not sure if you're on some reality television program. It was one of those times when you just pause for a second and look around trying to find the camera because you know you must be on Candid Camera or something like it. I was literally about two seconds from going totally and completely berserk, but somehow I channeled the composure to ask in a steady voice, "What am I supposed to do for the team poster if I don't have a uniform?"

"Well I don't know," he responded, brushing me off in that don't-bother-me-with-questions-about-equipment-even-though-I'm-the-equipment-manager-and-it's-my-job manner. I would come to find, in the subsequent months, that getting brushed off is something that I would have to get used to. Perhaps brushing off the walk-on is in the Boston College Athletics job description or perhaps it's one of the first few chapters in the training manual. Either way, it seemed to happen quite frequently.

I remember feeling totally downtrodden about the whole situation. I kept imagining how the poster would look and how I would not be a part of it. I envisioned Boston College students hanging it on their dorm room walls, proudly displaying their basketball team to the world, myself (probably non-conspicuously) absent from the picture. Naturally, the first thought that popped into my head was that maybe the coaches still weren't sure if I was going to make the team so they didn't want me to be in the poster picture just in case they decided to cut me after all. That was the only reasonable explanation I could think of. Why else would there just not be a jersey for me? And again, why was there only one pair of shoes in my locker the day before? After all, how difficult could it possibly be for a big-time ACC basketball program to get a basketball jersey and the correct number of pairs of shoes?

I slowly turned around and began to walk out of the equipment room and back up to the locker room, a sickening feeling of morose depression weighing down on me. I just kept trying to console myself. *"You knew this was going to be a difficult and trying experience. You knew this wouldn't be easy in the least bit. You knew you wouldn't get the same advantages and privileges as the rest of the guys. And most importantly, you knew you would have to deal with adversity."* Somehow, I still felt utterly blindsided. I felt like a boxer who had been dealt a first-round bulldozing, falling victim to a stiff right uppercut, out on my feet but somehow trying to keep my gloves in front of my face. I suppose despite the fact that I knew I'd meet with a bit of adversity at different points throughout the year, it just sent me for a loop when the first taste of hardship came this early in the campaign. I guess I just always assumed the major struggle I would have to deal with was the fact that I wasn't going to get much, if any, playing time. I think it was just difficult to swallow the fact that the season had yet to commence and I was already facing significant privation.

As I walked out from the equipment storage room, head down and depressed, I was surprised to hear Dave's voice call me back into the room where we were talking.

"I guess you can wear this uniform," he said, holding out a gold, number 10 Boston College Basketball jersey.

"Where did that come from?" I asked, not initially noticing how small the jersey was.

"It is a girls' uniform," he informed me. "A player on the girls' team wore it a couple of years ago. Laura Lokitis."

Sure enough, when he turned the jersey around, the name "Lokitis" was hemmed across the back. However, I had little choice in the matter, so I took the jersey and went back upstairs to the locker room. He did manage to find me a pair of men's shorts that actually fit me, however. While I was certainly grateful for the uniform because now I could be in the poster picture, I also knew that I was going to get a dose of ridicule from my teammates, who couldn't possibly let the fact that I was going to be wearing a women's jersey in the poster fly under the radar.

When I got back up to the locker room, I put on the gold shorts, my white Reeboks, and rather ashamedly, pulled on the too-small women's jersey displaying the name Lokitis. Literally seconds after the jersey fell on my shoulders, the chorus of jeers sounded in striking unison.

"Damn Brandon, that jersey is mad tight!"

"You been hittin' the weight room Brandon?"

"Your last name's Lokitis? Brandon Lokitis?"

Of course, when all the negative comments, ridiculing, jeers, jokes, jests, digs, witticisms, taunts, scoffs, and sneers were used up, there was the ever-popular fit of laughter as well. (I think now is a good time in my narrative to inform the reader of one of the most frustrating hardships I faced the entire year. Throughout my time in the Boston College Basketball program, almost every member of the team referred to me as "Brandon." For probably the first month of the season I continually corrected their ignorance when they would call me by this other name; however, as the weeks wore on, it became a fruitless struggle. Eventually, I simply gave in to the guys and let them refer to me by whatever name they chose. It was simply a battle I had neither the time nor energy to fight. Ironically, some of the guys on the team, namely John Oates and Tyler Roche, began calling me Brandon as a joke, making a small mockery of some of the other guys' obtuseness.)

As I entered the gym to take the poster pictures, I noticed a photography "booth" set up in the far corner of the gym. Each member of the team would take turns getting his picture taken. Each person was supposed to make three or four different poses, either holding a basketball or not. Some guys put the ball under their arms. Some put the ball under their feet. Some palmed the ball toward the camera. Others just crossed their arms or turned their back to the camera. When it was my turn to go, I kept my poses simple – just crossing my arms for one, holding the ball on my hip for one, and palming it behind my back for my third. I had to make sure to remember that I couldn't turn my back to the camera because my shirt read "Lokitis," rather than "Bennett." I also didn't want to let the camera see how the jersey I was wearing was so tight, unlike the jerseys everyone else was wearing. A week later when the posters arrived, I discovered that they decided to use the picture of me palming the ball behind my back. Everyone on the team grabbed a bunch of copies and everyone asked each other to sign their posters. I got three copies of the poster signed – one I gave to my high school English teacher, one I sent to my Boston College pen pal, and the other I framed and put on my wall at home, a visual testament to my accomplishment and a reminder that I can succeed in whatever I do.

Chapter XVI

Normal Practice

"Sometimes a player's greatest challenge is
coming to grips with his role on the team."

- Scottie Pippen

The day the posters came in and we took turns signing each other's posters was the last time I felt like I was part of the team. From that moment on, I felt like I was an outsider looking in – like that lonesome raven once again, flying just below the rest of the team.

As the season opener against New Hampshire approached, our practice schedule became quite routine. Almost every day our practice would consist of the same drills and activities. I'd arrive at the gym at around 1:30 to warm up, stretch, and get some shots up before practice. At 2:00 – our every-day practice time – one of the coaches would enter the gym and blow the whistle, which instructed us to begin lay-up lines.

One aspect of Boston College practices that I always thought was interesting was that everything we ever did was timed by one of our team managers using the scoreboard clock. Lay-up lines would last 10 minutes and when the horn sounded, we'd move on to the next drill. Of course, before we could move on to the next drill, anyone who missed a lay-up (as I did the first day of practice) had to run. If we missed one lay-up or shot, we had to run a suicide in 28 seconds (Coach referred to these as "28s") and if we missed two lay-ups, we had to run a feezy in one minute (which Coach called "full-court 5s"). It was a pretty safe bet that someone would miss at least one lay-up each day.

After lay-up lines, Coach would yell, "Line 'em up," or "On the line," and whoever missed would have to run. Most days, when only one person would miss a lay-up, someone else on the team would run with him – sort of a "good teammate" gesture. I, however, always wary of burning myself out before practice really began, never ran with anyone on the team – except Tyrelle, because he ran with me on the first day of practice (but he rarely missed). For the first few days of practice, especially after I missed two on the first day, I was very careful not to miss even a single lay-up. I would put painstaking care into each shot, afraid that I'd have to make the embarrassing run another time. However, after a few weeks of never having to run again, Coach Murphy approached me before practice one day and told me that I should be running with the guys whenever possible. He said it would be appropriate as the walk-on to run every sprint with the team. From then on, while most of the guys would laugh or make a joke when someone missed a lay-up and had to run, I always hated seeing it happen because I knew that I had to run with that person.

As the season wore on and guys were getting into better and better shape because games were underway, they would have contests during lay-up lines – like a basketball version of the game Chicken – where they would take turns launching three-pointers instead of taking sure-make lay-ups, until one person would miss and that person would have to run. I dreaded this game because it almost guaranteed that I'd have to run with someone that day. Sometimes, it even meant that I'd have to run a feezy because the same person might miss twice, this early feezy typically guaranteeing me "lead-legs" for the rest of practice.

Most days, we would "dummy" our offense for 10 minutes or so before Coach Skinner entered the gym. We would run half-speed through each of our man-to-man offensive sets, making sure every player knew every position he would be in. Following man sets, we'd move into the few zone sets we had and finish with out-of-bounds plays, which we had quite a few of. This part of practice became relatively mundane for me, namely because I was often not one of the five players on the court. We had 13 guys on our roster and we'd dummy on both ends of the court, meaning that 10 guys would be dummying offense at a time. Some days, when the first 10 had sufficiently run through the plays, I would be allowed to work on a few plays for the last few minutes; however, I never really had the chance to learn all of the plays from all of the positions (though I would probably never find myself in any position other than the point guard or the shooting guard).

After lay-ups, the team would move to a full-court drill called the three-man-weave to further loosen the muscles. This drill involves three players running the length of the court, one player passing the ball to a teammate, running behind him (following the ball), and then catching the ball from the third teammate and repeating the process until they all reach the other end of the court. However, unlike any three-man-weave I had ever been a part of, this weave didn't end with a lay-up or jump shot, but rather, a dunk. It was a rule of the drill that one of the three players had to end the weave with a dunk. If the threesome didn't end the drill with a dunk they had to start over and do it again. Naturally, any group that I was in was at a distinct disadvantage because I can rarely dunk. However, I would position myself strategically to run with groups in which I knew there was a guy who could easily dunk or a guy who wanted to do the dunking, as to avoid having to try to dunk myself.

Immediately following lay-up lines and three-man-weave, Coach Skinner would make us run sprints as a team for the previous game's turnovers. If we had fewer than 16 turnovers, we didn't have to run. If we had 16 turnovers we had to run a 28, and each time the number reached another multiple of 2, i.e. 18, 20, 22, etc., we had to tack on a feezy. Some particularly sloppy games might include upwards of 20 turnovers, ultimately leading to a great amount of running at the beginning of practice. Again, for a player who doesn't get much game time, or practice time for that matter, this much running can make one's legs feel heavy rather quickly.

The next time slot at practice usually consisted of one of two drills. Some days we would do a drill called "five on zero," in which we would work on our fast break and secondary break offenses (parts of the game I had never been exposed to before and were literally unaware of). We would do a sort of five-man-weave down the length of the court and work on a series of offenses, typically ending the drill by running flex, our primary offensive set, through a couple of times and getting a lay-up. Again, like most drills, I would be allowed to participate some days, but not others. Some days I would be allowed the run the point for the third group, but some days, typically when we had a complete roster, meaning no one was hurt, sick, or in trouble with grades, I would just watch or take free throws on one of the side baskets.

The other drill that sometimes occupied this spot was a five-on-five press/press break drill. We would work on the fundamentals of breaking a press and transitioning into an offense situation. This was a drill I rarely, if ever, was allowed to participate in because it involved full scrimmaging.

Next, we would have a shooting session, called "two on a ball," in which the team would break up into six groups of two and shoot at the six baskets with a partner. However, if my reader hadn't noticed, groups of two people at six baskets only adds up to 12 players. I being the 13th player would unfortunately have to join a group, making it a threesome, which meant fewer shots for me. Moreover, what was more so the issue was that my presence at a basket meant fewer shots for the guys who mattered (harsh as it may sound, it was true, and I eventually accepted that as my role). This session typically consisted of the players putting up a series of shots in two-minute increments and then rebounding for the other player for the next two minutes, etc. During the last four minutes, the two players would shoot only three-pointers and keep track of their totals, trying to improve every day. While I was permitted to shoot for one of the two-minute increments, I was never allowed to shoot during the last four minutes.

After two on a ball, we usually moved into a drill called "shell drill." Shell is a four-on-four or five-on-five half-court, game-like scenario in which we would run our man sets against our teammates and keep track of the points (obviously when we ran four-on-four, we couldn't run plays, so we just screened and cut). Points could only be scored by making a basket (some coaches like to award points for offensive rebounds, defensive stops, charges, etc.), so each offensive possession was important. Like every competitive drill we did during practice, the loser, or losing team in this case, would have to run a 28 or a feezy, depending on the severity of the loss. I was usually allowed to play shell, especially when we only had 12 guys at practice because Coach often preferred to run four-on-four.

After shell, we would do a free throw shooting drill called "40 out of 50." For this drill, the team would split up into two groups of six (one of seven), and each team would go to one of the main hoops. Each player would take turns shooting free throws – like a one-and-one scenario – until each team had put up 25 shots. The goal of the drill was to make 40 out of 50 as a team. If we were unable to make the mark, we would have to run a feezy. This drill was a personal adversary of mine because of the pressure I put on myself. If I missed a free throw, I would feel like the team was running because of me, and I always felt like I was at an unfair disadvantage because I was often cold when I shot (cold meaning that I had been sitting out for a while and my muscles were tight or literally cold). Also, some of my teammates would make it seem like it was my fault if we had to run. Despite the fact that we shot an abysmal 69% from the charity stripe during the season, it was often "my fault" when we had to run.

After 40 out of 50, we moved into a drill called "miss/make." Miss/make was the focal point of our practices, occupying most of our practice time. It was a five-on-five 20-minute, running-time scrimmage in which we would get a real sense of how our offenses worked and how our personnel worked together. We always kept score during this drill, and like every other drill, the losing team would have to run. If the team lost by six or fewer points, they would have to run a 28; however, if they lost by seven or more, they would run a feezy. One of the unspoken goals of the drill was to make the other team run as much as possible, so if one team was winning by four with a few seconds left, they would always try to make a three-pointer to make the other team run a feezy. This was a drill I was extremely rarely allowed to participate in and I would have to stand on the sideline for the entire 20 minutes. However, like during lay-up line running, when the losing team would line up to run, I would have to run with them, despite which team lost. Naturally, I would hope that the losing team would be able to lose by fewer than seven so I would only have to run a suicide.

Immediately following miss/make, we would do another set of 40 out of 50, run if we were unable to reach our goal, and then jump right back into another 20-minute session of miss/make, during which I would again stand on the sideline.

As the year progressed, I remained optimistic about my role on the team and tried to convince myself that eventually I would be able to show the coaches that I could play and that I certainly, if nothing else, belonged as an integral member during practice. However, as the season wore on and more and more games came and went, I found myself becoming more and more negative. I would stand on the sideline, watching my teammates run through drills and scrimmages, only having a chance to play when someone would get hurt or when we needed an extra body because someone had to miss practice. Some days, I would stand alone for almost the complete two hours. Most of the time, I was not even a part of the practice at all.

What's worse was the way I felt forced to speak of my situation on the team as if it were the cliché, "feel-good" story. People would say, "Wow, you must be having the time of your life! That must be awesome to be a part of the team!" Reporters would call my house, asking, "Did you ever think a 6' kid from Central Mass. would get the chance to play D1 ball at BC? Aren't you just reveling in each and every moment?"

"Oh yes," I would respond. "It's truly an unbelievable experience." In truth, however, it was nothing but a dreadfully lonely experience.

Chapter XVII
Pre-Game Routine

"Today's preparation determines tomorrow's achievement."

- Unknown Author

As the weeks of practice leading up to our first game against New Hampshire finally ended I was overcome with a sense of relief. I had begun to feel like I was not really a part of the team and I was glad to see our first game fast approaching, hoping that with it would come a heightened sense of camaraderie among my teammates.

Two days before our first game, we had our first preparatory film session of the year after the day's practice. During this film session, or any other of the 31 film sessions we would have (31 games), one of our assistant coaches would review each of the opposing team's starting players (the assistant coaches had a rotation in which they would take turns scouting the teams we were going to play and going over the scout during film sessions). Coach would review each of the starters' strengths and weaknesses, telling us everything we could possible hope to know about each player. We would be informed about how many points he scores, how many assists he averages, his turnover numbers, his free throw percentage, his offensive and defensive tendencies, etc., all while watching a series of individual video clips on each opposing player. Furthermore, we would learn who would be guarding each player and the coaches would try to help our guys understand the best ways to stop certain players and the best ways to attack them offensively.

The next day, one day before our game, we would get the video scout on the rest of the team's personnel, typically players who come off the bench but still get significant minutes. After all of the personnel were drilled into our heads, we would move on to the other team's offensive sets. Our coaches would break down each and every offensive play the other team has, trying to teach us the best way to beat the offense. We would learn what each of the other team's hand signals meant and also how teams get into their secondary break offenses (for example, North Carolina has their point guard do a spin dribble just over half court signaling to the rest of the players that a particular play is called). Finally, we would learn about the types of defenses and defensive pressure the other team primarily runs. We would be told if the other team plays mostly man-to-man or if they like to drop back into a zone and whether or not they press full-court, and if so, what type of press they run (man-to-man, 2-2-1 full-court, 1-2-1-1 full-court, 1-3-1 half-court, etc.).

The practice on the day before a game was always an easy one. It would typically last a little more than an hour, rather than the usual 2+ hours. We would usually not do any really intensive basketball activities on those days – mostly just shooting and scout. We would often begin in normal fashion with lay-up lines and three-man-weave, then move into some light basketball drilling – shell drill perhaps.

There were a few drills we only did on day-before-a-game practices, however. We would do one drill called "make 85," in which we had three minutes to make 85 baskets. The team divided into two groups, one on each end of the court, and then further subdivided into three lines on each end. Ultimately, what the drill consisted of was each player running the length of the court for a jump shot or lay-up. If we didn't reach 85, we would have to do the drill again until we made it.

Another drill we would do was called "full-court shooting." Full-court shooting was a drill which involved the team once again splitting into two groups, one at each basket. One of the managers would set the clock for 6 minutes. During the first minute, we had to run the length of the court while dribbling the basketball and make a right handed lay-up. Once we got to the other end of the floor, we had to get our rebound and when we got to the front of the line, we had to do the same thing coming back down the court. After the first minute, we had to shoot an elbow jump shot. During the third minute, we had to shoot a three-pointer. Once the first three minutes were up, we switched sides and went from the left side. This drill was always fun because I would have a shooting contest with John Oates, Tyler Roche, and Joe Trapani to see who could score the most points – 1 for a lay-up, 2 for an elbow jumper, and 3 for a three-pointer. It always gave me a sense of accomplishment if I could beat them – though I think it might have only happened once.

The day-before-a-game practice would conclude the same way each time – with scout team. Scout team at Boston College is the same concept as scout team in high school basketball or football. The last five guys on the team – on this particular team it was Cortney Dunn, Daye Kaba, Joe Trapani (because he couldn't play because he transferred), usually Josh Southern, and myself – would come out and run through the other team's offensive sets. While we covered them extensively in film that day before practice, it is always easier to comprehend something when it is done in front of you. After we ran through their plays a few times, Coach would put the starting five on defense to guard us. We would walk through the plays and they would learn where they had to be at certain times.

Scout team always aroused strange feelings for me. On the one hand, I knew I was only out there on scout team because I was one of the five weakest players on the team. On the other hand, however, I felt down deep that I was out there because I could be like the guy I was imitating. I felt like I could be just as good as that player (which is absolutely absurd because I was pretending to be guys like Ty Lawson and Greg Paulus). Perhaps it was the feeling of having everyone's eyes on me, watching me run through the other team's plays, which created this false feeling in me. Throughout my entire career, from my earliest exposure to basketball at the age of five or six through my dominance at the high school level, I always had the eyes on me. I was always the one making the plays, scoring the baskets, and winning the game for my team. However, now, for the first time in my career, there were no eyes on me. For the first time in my career, I was the worst player on the team.

Imagine that... Take whatever it is that you are good at, perhaps what you are the best at, and suddenly imagine yourself as the worst at it. Imagine yourself completely unable to compete at what you have always been the best. It is a hard pill to swallow. I really attribute that strange feeling in the pit of my stomach to the fact that at BC I no longer got the attention I had always received and for those brief 10 minutes, when the eyes were on me, I felt valued again – even if I knew it was untrue.

I think it is important to point out the great amount of preparation Coach Skinner and his staff put into each game. I have played for a lot of different coaches throughout my career and many of them have done significant pre-game analysis of other teams; however, none has ever even come remotely close to the depth in which Coach Skinner and his assistants prepared us. The film we watched was unlike any film I have ever watched. We had multiple highlight clips of not only each player and set, but of each point and detail the coaches were trying to convey. Furthermore, we delved extensively into scout team, sometimes spending almost 20 minutes walking through every play the other team would run. Every basketball coach in the world has his or her own set of strengths. Some are great motivators. Some are excellent recruiters. Others are superior game planners. Some just have that sixth sense and can predict what the other team is going to do. Coach Skinner's greatest strength, in my opinion, is his ability to prepare a team for a game. Many people criticize Coach Skinner for different things like his lack of intensity or his unwillingness to abandon the flex offense and adapt to the ACC style of play; however, if these people could experience what I have experienced, they would see that his strengths don't lay in his intensity like a Bob Knight or in his ability to adapt to a new league like a Roy Williams. Coach Skinner's strengths are of the unseen variety, with his capacity to prepare for a game as his foremost talent.

*****

The last type of practice we would have in the Boston College Basketball program was a pre-game practice which we would have on the day of the game. These practices tended to be very short, only maybe 45 minutes or so, and were more like walk-throughs than actual practices. Pre-game practices would usually begin with what we called "guard/forward shooting." Basically, this drill comes as advertised. The guards would go to one end of the floor and the forwards and centers would go to the other and just put up a bunch of shots. We would take a number of shots – lay-ups, jumpers, pull-ups, and three-pointers. We would also take some shots after catching the ball from a pass from one of the assistant coaches.

After guard/forward shooting, we would occasionally do a full-court shooting contest between two teams. Coach would split the team into two units and each player would have to dribble the length of the court and shoot a shot from the elbow or foul line. If he missed the shot, he had to get his rebound and shoot again. Once he made the shot, he had to run back down the floor and make the same shot on the other hoop. Once he made this shot, he could give the ball to the next guy in line and he had to do the same. The first team to have everyone make the two shots was the winner. While there was no punishment for not winning this contest, everyone was extremely competitive and would hassle the other team to try to get them to miss. Naturally, the more times a player missed the shot, the more he was ridiculed, and consequently, the more he would miss the shot. It truly is a vicious circle. I attribute everyone's readiness to ridicule teammates to the simple fact that everyone on the team has an extremely competitive nature and wants to win so badly at everything they do – I suppose if you're playing Division I basketball you literally have to have a competitive nature.

After the shooting contest, we would break into two groups – guards on one end and bigs on the other – and take turns shooting two free throws at a time. We would shoot for five minutes at the first hoop and then switch baskets for five more minutes. I always liked the few minutes we would shoot free throws because after we shot the two shots, we would go up for a lay-up and get "boosted up" by two of our teammates. Two of the guys under the hoop, usually Tyler Roche and Tyrese Rice, would grab me by the waist and literally throw me up towards the rim. This would give me about an extra foot of vertical leap and I would be able to do some fun dunks. It was always funny to see guys who can dunk easily anyway get boosted.

The last thing we would do during pre-game practices is another shooting game which Coach simply called "shooting game." Once again, we would be broken into two teams, however, this time, both teams started on the same hoop, each team in a line at one of the two elbows.

Each player would take turns shooting until the team reached 10 baskets. After a team made 10 shots, they would move the line to the wing, where they had to make 10 17-foot jumpers. After they made these 10, they would move to the baseline to try to make 10 more. After the team completed all three spots, they had to sprint down to the other end of the court and complete the same three spots. The hardest part of the drill was not making the shots, but rather, getting the rebound and getting the ball to the next guy in line. Once the shot was up, it was literally a free-for-all. The guy from the other team who shot at the same time as you could get in your way, hit your ball, or deflect your ball, as long as it was "unintentional," though it was very rarely unintentional. If Coach deemed the play to be an infraction, meaning the guy hit your ball on purpose, he would penalize the entire team and let the other team get three free shots. Tyler Roche was particularly good at knocking the ball away while still making it look like an accident. Sometimes, if a guy was intentionally getting in the way of another guy, he would just throw the ball into the guy's face or chest to teach him a lesson to not get in his way again. Understandably, this game could and would get a little violent.

After one team finished all six spots, making 10 shots at each location, they had to run back down to the other end and make eight consecutive free throws. The first team to make the eight free throws was the winner. Naturally, the free throws could take a while – as I already stated, we were a 69% free throw shooting team. Some guys on the team always felt like they had something to prove and would have to be the one to make the last two. I, on the other hand, was quite content taking care of the first or second pair, and escaping a bit of the mockery. Though Shamari Spears was never light on the scorn no matter when I shot in the course of the eight free throws. I could hear him at half court (the "mockers" were not allowed to step over half court) yelling, "Hey Brandon! You ain't gonna make this shot! Look at that stupid ass hair." (For most of the season I had relatively long hair.) Basically, anything the guys could find to insult you with, they would use. It could be anything from the clothes you wore, to the style of your hair, to the type of boots you had, to the type of grades you got, etc. One particular joke they would often make was about one of the guy's hairline. They would just tease him nonstop about how his hairline was not neat. It was almost laughable the types of things guys could come up with.

After we finally finished the shooting game, we would bring it in and Coach would talk a little about the upcoming game. After he was finished talking, we would go up to the Shea room, which was upstairs in Conte Forum, and eat a pre-game meal. The pre-game meal was always great for me because it was free and meant that I didn't have to buy lunch or use my student account money in the dining hall. The athletic department would serve us a plethora of food, ranging from soup to steak, fish to potatoes, and salad to cake. I would always grab a few extra juices and bring them back to my room. If our game was early, like a 1:00 p.m. start, we would have a pre-game breakfast which consisted of omelets, waffles, hash browns, and anything else one would eat at breakfast. Coach always wanted to make sure that we ate a good, full meal before each game so we would have energy to compete at a high level. We ate the same way on the road, eating a pre-game meal in a banquet hall at whatever hotel we were staying at.

After our games, when we got back to the locker room, we would be given food again – this time it was always either pizza or subs. The amount of free food I got, either during pre-game meals or post-game meals, was just another one of the great benefits of being a member of the Boston College Basketball team.

Chapter XVI

A Day at Children's H

"The life of a man consists not in seeing visions and in dreaming dreams, but in active charity and in willing service."

- Henry Wadsworth Longfellow

One off-day, early in the season, our entire team went to the cancer ward of Children's Hospital in Boston to spend the day with the terminally ill children. When we got to Children's Hospital, we were instructed to wait in the waiting room, none of us really knowing what we were going to be doing or how we were going to be interacting with the children, if at all. As we were waiting, a woman came to speak with us about how we would spend our day. She told us that we would be splitting up into groups of five or six and the groups would be going to different floors of the hospital and talking with different kids. Before the two groups split up, however, she asked for two volunteers to go with her and dress up and perform a short skit for some children. I remember Cortney Dunn was particularly excited to do the show.

When the nurse who was leading us around the floor led my group, which consisted of Tyler Roche, John Oates, Rakim Sanders, Coach Skinner, and myself, into the first room, I was a little nervous for what I would encounter. I'm not sure what it was about the idea of visiting and interacting with terminally ill children that made me uneasy. For some reason, I felt like they would judge me in a negative way. I felt like they would look at my teammates and me and hate us or be cold to us because of what we had, however, to my surprise, and my delight, quite the opposite was true. Each and every room we went into, and each and every child we met with and talked to was absolutely radiant upon meeting us. Every kid looked at us with glowing eyes and big, wide smiles and asked us a million and one questions. *"What's it like*

*tball in college? Do you know Tyrese? Do you play against North
nd Duke?"* My favorite question is one of the most popular –
u dunk?" After the child's initial shock of seeing us wore off and
r she finished the torrent of questions, we would offer him or her
e of our team posters which everyone on the team autographed for
the kids. Upon receiving this gift, each child would only smile wider,
and subsequently, I would smile broader, too.

I specifically remember one little boy who was so happy to receive
the poster from us that he jumped out of bed and ran over to his shelf
to put the poster next to an autographed football. I asked him about the
football and he and his father told us a story about how Adalius
Thomas, a linebacker for the New England Patriots, had visited him the
day before and signed the ball (and the father's hat) especially for him.
All I could do was stand and smile as he rambled on about the two
autographed items he had collected, but truthfully, the joy he displayed
was well-worth any amount of listening I had to do. As we left the little
boy's room, the nurse told us that Thomas had come visit him because
he was the boy's favorite player and the boy didn't have much time left.
When someone tells you something like that – something devastating
about someone who you just spoke with and spent time with – you feel
like you have been hit in the stomach by the heavyweight champion of
the world. You feel like the air has been sucked out of the room and
you fight just to catch your breath. When the nurse told us that that boy
only had a few days, maybe a week, left, I just wanted to leave the
hospital. Nothing in the world can ever prepare you to hear news like
that. My heart goes out to the parents of these children who have to,
God forbid, hear news like that someday.

On a more positive note, however, it was amazing to see the way
those kids would light up when we entered the room. The whole
experience was almost surreal for me. I kept asking myself questions
about how these kids could smile and talk with us with such exuberance
despite the fact that they were so sick. How could they find such joy in
talking to a bunch of college basketball players, when the God-honest
truth is that most of the team really didn't want to be there at all?
Words cannot express the feeling of importance I felt on that day. The
fact that my presence in that hospital brightened the life of a child who

doesn't have a whole lot to smile about brings me a sense of pride like nothing else I have ever done.

After we went into most of the rooms on the floor, the nurse took my group down to the recreation center where the kids did most of their physical activity. She brought us to a basketball gym where a group of children were shooting around and playing tag. She told us that we could play basketball with the kids, but that we needed to remember to take it easy on them. When we first entered the gym, most of the kids, except for a few brave ones, remained on the far end of the court. My teammates picked up a basketball and began to shoot in a group among themselves, but I wanted to interact with the children a little more. I walked over to the other basket, where they were shooting, and began to rebound for them, offering brief bits of encouragement and praise for their efforts. After a while, I told some of the kids to go down to the other end of the court and play with the guys on the team, and some of them obliged. I remember two little girls, in particular, who stayed down on my end and asked me to play them two-on-one. Of course they won the game, but to me it wasn't a loss I was overly worried about. The fact that they got to have a good time with someone they thought was a big deal (whether or not being the walk-on at BC makes me a big deal or not is irrelevant), was all the victory I needed.

I have to admit that I was slightly unprepared for our day in the cancer ward. I have never been exposed to terminally ill children, and the experience was "grounding," in a word. That day really made me appreciate what I have in life, the family and friends I am blessed with, and the health of all those I love, which is so often taken for granted. That day rewarded me with a renewed sense of the importance of each day, each experience, and each moment I share with those I love, and opened my eyes to what is really important in life – living each moment as if it were your last.

104 • Colle...
104
Whe...
added ...
work...
N...

Chapter XIX

The Weight Room

"Good, better, best. Never let it rest.
Until your good is better and your better is best."

– Tim Duncan

One of the most important elements of becoming an efficient and effective basketball player is strength training. Throughout my basketball career, until I began my tenure with the Boston College Eagles, I had never truly delved into the world of strength training. Like most athletes, I had always put great effort into my physical fitness by implementing a daily exercise routine into my life, including a daily two-mile run and nightly push-ups and sit-ups. However, because I played three sports, meaning I would be occupied during the three seasons of the school year (football in the fall, basketball in the winter, and baseball in the spring), I was reluctant to lift during the school year, in the fear that I would throw off my shot, swing, or speed. However, again, like most high school athletes, I strength trained with weights during the summer months, but no amount of individual strength training I could do would prepare me for the types of strength training I would encounter at Boston College.

During my freshman year at BC, I would often work out in the Plex on days when I wouldn't play pick-up basketball, doing a few sets of bench presses, curls, triceps extensions, and shoulder presses, but never doing any leg strength work. However, as I began my career with Boston College Basketball, I learned that the college's athletes have the privilege of using a private (only available to student-athletes), state-of-the-art weight room. On top of the ability to use the weight room whenever I wanted, I was also privy to any knowledge that any of the three strength coaches – Nick, Tom, and Russ – could offer me.

n I first walked into the weight room after my name was o the roster (I was forbidden from using the weight room or ing out with the team until I was officially on the roster due to AA rules), I was astonished at the number of fitness machines there were. In the center of the room were five bench press complexes, complete with benches, bars, and overhanging towers to hold the weight plates. Directly behind the bench press towers, facing the opposite direction, as if standing back-to-back, were five squat towers. Along the far wall of the room were four squat assist machines, which Nick referred to as "bear squat" machines. These machines allowed athletes to do squats to increase leg strength without having to worry about having a spotter. Along the side wall on the right side of the room, near the bear squat machines, were four seated row machines and four lat pull towers. Along the other side wall, on the left side of the room, were a long row of free weights, ranging from five-pound dumbbells to 100-pound weights. Finally, directly to the left of the door, were a number of cardio machines, ranging from treadmills to elliptical machines and bikes to Stairmasters.

Every day when we would come into the weight room to lift after practice, the first thing we were required to do was get a stretch from one of the strength coaches. One of the worst "crimes" we could commit in the weight room was to pull a muscle because we didn't stretch properly, and for a guy like me who isn't blessed with a lot of flexibility, stretching is simply a must. The stretching routine was extremely effective, giving me a great stretch on the inner hamstring, groin, hip flexor, hamstring, gluteus, calves, and lower back. After the stretch from the coach, I would always do a quick quadriceps stretch because for some reason, unbeknownst to me, the quadriceps were conspicuously absent from the stretching regimen.

It consistently confounds me that I have become so tight and inflexible as I have gotten older. While I was never an overly flexible or limber person, I can never remember being as tight as I am now. I can remember being a kid and running out onto the court without even having stretched first, yet never worrying about pulling a muscle or enduring an injury. During high school I always made sure to stretch, but I could finish exercising and not immediately tighten back up.

Likewise, never before had it taken me so long to loosen up in the first place. Even after stretching before practice, it still takes me 10 or 15 minutes of light jogging and jumping to really feel ready to play at a high, competitive level. Similarly, when we would have morning practices, it would take me an incredibly long time to loosen up before practice. Never before in my career had I ever had to deal with this necessity for serious pre-practice stretching, loosening up, and muscle preparation.

However, this fact leads me to one of the most important lessons I learned early in my Boston College career: it is imperative to know your body – and know it well. If it takes you a few minutes to stretch before doing physical activity, then it is of utmost importance to take these few minutes to stretch appropriately and avoid injury. If it takes you 15 minutes to stretch and then 15 more minutes to jog lightly, like me, then again, it is extremely valuable to your athletic success to do so. On the same note, if you do sustain an injury during play, it is again important to know your own body and understand how long it'll take to recuperate and what healing methods – ice, heat, etc. – are best to help your particular injury. Finally, one absolutely crucial thing to understand about your body is how it will react to certain amounts of sleep and how naps can affect your athletic performance. Knowing your body is one of the major cornerstones to being a successful athlete.

As a member of the Boston College Basketball team, I was required to complete a weekly lifting regimen, which was displayed on the coaches white board near the front of the room, outside of their offices. The lifting chart would be organized by day (typically four lifts per week) and then broken down into specific lifts on each day. Typically, each day's major lift would be either bench presses or squats, as these two exercises are thought to be two of the most integral strength training lifts. The other lifts would include curls, triceps work, shoulder presses, rows, lat-pull-downs, and hanging abdominal lifts. Displayed under each lift was also the amount of sets, the percentage of our "max weight" we were to lift during each set, and the number of reps we were to complete with the exercise, as well. (Our max weight was calculated on the first day we lifted as a team. We attempted to bench press a certain amount and if we were able to put up the weight successfully, we added five or 10 pounds and attempted to lift it again. We kept repeating this process until the weight was too much to lift. The weight on the bar during the rep before we could not lift it another time was our max.) For example:

Bench Press					
Percent of Max:	65%	75%	80%	85%	95%
Reps:	10	7	5	3	1

At the beginning of the season, my max weight was determined to be 220 pounds, so for this particular example, I would have to do 10 reps at 65% of 220 pounds, which is 143 pounds, which we would always round up to 145 pounds. The second set I would have to do seven reps at 165 pounds, etc. I found this lifting program to be extremely successful and by the end of the academic year – after eight months of lifting with routines like the aforementioned one – my max weight had increased from 220 pounds to 245 pounds.

One of the best perks of being a basketball player and working out in the private weight room was that we were given protein bars and muscle recovery milkshakes after workouts. I heard from other athletes that basketball and hockey were the only sports that were given free bars and shakes. Other student-athletes who wanted them had to buy their own. Basketball players were also allowed to have as many free Powerade drinks as we wanted during weight room sessions.

It always surprised me that many of my teammates were reluctant to work out, while others simply refused to do so altogether. I suppose I understand their logic very well, it being that they simply didn't want to upset their "basketball equilibrium," meaning that they didn't want to affect their shots or jumping abilities by lifting too heavily. It seemed like the guys who got the most playing time were also the ones who lifted the least frequently. Guys like me, who got almost no playing time at all, were the ones who lifted the most often. I always lifted at least four times a week, sometimes five or even six times. I tried to squat at least three times a week, and by the end of the season, I definitely noticed a big difference in my strength, especially when trying to box out a bigger and stronger player than me or when trying to prevent a player from cutting through the lane unabated. I suppose it was only beneficial for me to be in the weight room as much as possible.

One particular lifting experience stands out in my mind because as I went into the weight room to bench press one Saturday, I noticed that Boston Red Sox gold glove first baseman, Kevin Youkilis, was lifting in our weight room, too. I learned that the weight room at Fenway Park was under construction and he needed a place close by to lift, and to my surprise, it was at BC. I think it is important for my reader to understand the extreme nature of my Red Sox fanhood. As I've said, during the summer, when the Sox lose a game, my whole day is affected. I will refuse to watch Sportscenter that night and just feel emotionally low when the Sox don't play well. So for a Sox fan like me to see one of the "local nine" in my weight room, it was quite a thrill. I remember between sets of bench presses (mind you Youk was lifting on the bench directly next to me), I ran up to the locker room and grabbed my cell phone. Without being overly obvious and sticking the cell phone in his face, I snapped a few candid photos of him and quickly sent them to some of my friends, gloating about my close proximity to a member of the Red Sox.

*****

Another aspect of training that the strength coaches did with us outside the weight room was vertical leap measurements and speed and quickness tests. At the beginning of the season, the coaches wanted to take these measurements and then after the basketball season (and a season of lifting and intense exercise), we would retest and hopefully increase in all areas.

The first test we did was a straight vertical leap test. Each person would stand flatfooted under a tower of markers, each one about half an inch apart. Before we jumped, we had to reach our hand straight up as far as it could go, marking the highest point of our reach. Then we were instructed to bend our knees and jump straight up, reaching our hand as high as possible. Our vertical leap would ultimately be calculated by subtracting the initial reach from the highest point we could reach during our jump. The highest point we could reach would be calculated by determining what the highest colored marker our finger could touch was. These markers would spin horizontally around the center pole of the tower and the highest marker that spun around would be determined as our highest reach point. This is an effective leaping test because it measures the pure vertical leap, rather than just how high a player can reach on the basket. In other words, my vertical leap, which was between 28 and 30 inches, could be more than a 6' 6" player who only leaps 26 inches, but who can easily dunk a basketball.

The next test we did was a speed and quickness test using very high-tech body sensors. We had to line up on the baseline, under the hoop, and press our back foot on a sensor that would start the clock as soon as our foot was lifted off of it. We would then sprint from the original baseline toward the opposite baseline, having our time measured at two different locations – the first foul line (15 feet) and at half court (45 feet). The first measurement would primarily serve to define one's quickness, while the second mark illustrates one's overall speed. This concept is similar to sprinting during a track meet. When a sprinter wins the 100-meter sprint, one might comment that that runner is very fast. However, when one wins a 10-meter sprint (had this race been run), one might instead comment that that runner is very quick. If I had to define myself, I would certainly say that I am extremely quick, but not overly fast in longer sprints. As I have already made clear, my first step (in other words, my initial quickness) is my greatest asset on the basketball court. Naturally, when my measurement at the first sensor (foul line) was returned, it proved to be one of the quickest times of anyone on the team – a time similar to that of Tyrese Rice and Daye Kaba. However, at the second sensor, my time became slower, more like one of our big guys. Every guy on the team got very competitive with this test, though the main goal of the exercise was to be able to beat our own times five months later.

One final test we did was a test to determine our overall body fat percentage. To calculate this percentage, we had to climb into an egg-shaped machine called the "Bod Pod." The front of the machine opened up like the doors of a Lamborghini, vertically, we climbed in and sat on a small ledge, and just as it opened, the door – more the front half of the machine – closed down, sealing us inside. We were instructed to sit as still as possible while inside the machine to receive the most accurate results. I never truly understood the science behind the Bod Pod, because when I sat inside it, there was a series of beeps, and just like that, the test was over. I expected to be bombarded with intense wind currents or squeezed by the walls like some full-body blood pressure test; however, there was nothing like that at all. When the test was over, I was told that my body fat percentage was 8.6%. The man who was running the tests told me that for my frame and height, I could probably drop this percentage to about 8% and bring my weight up to about 195 pounds, but anything over those amounts would not be optimal.

*****

As soon as the season was over, we began a lifting regimen which combined strength training with rapid repetition lifts, a process called metabolics. Metabolics is a type of lifting program which serves to train athletes in the exact same intensity levels they would expect to see during games or competitions. During most competitive sports, athletes engage in periods of extremely intense activity, typically followed by relatively equal periods of almost no activity, or total rest. For example, during a basketball game, a player might be running and jumping for a straight five or six minutes, but then that player might come out of the game and sit on the bench for five minutes. Metabolic training causes the body's metabolism to increase, burning significantly more calories and fat, while producing muscle. During this lifting program, we had to lift a weight, our 60% maximum weight, for example, as many times as we possibly could in a given amount of time, typically 30-45 seconds, simulating game-like intensity. For example, I would have to bench press 135 pounds as many times as possible in a 30-second period. During these lift days, we always lifted with a partner and when the clock at the front of the weight room reached zero (it would count down from a given time) and the buzzer would sound, we would switch and our partner would begin his period of lifting. Our partner would lift for the same amount of time, doing as many repetitions as he could, all the while the first person would rest. Like normal workout days, we would perform a series of lifts, including bench presses, squats, bicep curls, shoulder presses, rows, etc., but each was done in the metabolic form. This type of lifting produced extremely positive results very quickly; however, our strength coach would only allow us to do the metabolic lift for two weeks. He said that it isn't good for the muscles to be lifting that hard all the time. Eventually, one's body would break down if he continually performed this type of lift. Also, he said that the body reaches a point where it no longer responds in the same way to that type of rigorous workout. In other words, the muscles adjust to that type of strenuous activity, reaching a "plateau," and the results would no longer be as dramatic.

To this day, I feel like my time spent in the weight room at Boston College was one of the most impactful experiences in my athletic career – perhaps just as important as my time on the BC Basketball courts. In the weight room, I learned a great deal about strength training that I continually implement into my workout routines today, but moreover, I learned a great deal about my own body and the way it responds to certain exercises, stretches, and diets. I now know that I cannot lift the day before a game or I will feel tired and my muscles will feel heavy during my game. Furthermore, I learned that I cannot overdo certain lifts, like squats, because while they may supplement my vertical leap or overall strength, they also take a toll on my knees and hips. I learned that it is extremely important to stay within one's self in the weight room, as well, because what is right or beneficial for one person's body may be entirely harmful for mine. Also, I learned the importance of a complete body stretch before intense athletic activity. Now, before I begin warming-up for a game or before I lift or go out running, I always take 10-20 minutes to sufficiently stretch my body to avoid muscle pulls or other injuries. Finally, I learned the overall importance of eating properly and having a healthy diet. I'm not the type of person who believes in completely weaning one's self off of chips, candy, and other junk foods, but I do believe that it is beneficial for one's body to minimize the intake of these types of foods and try to eat healthily. Knowing my body the way I do, I know the ways certain foods will affect me. For instance, while some people love to load up on carbohydrates before athletic activity, i.e. eating pasta, I always feel negatively affected eating significant amounts of carbs before I play, so instead, I stick to a deli meat sandwich or sub. My understanding of each of these important aspects of personal health – strength training, stretching, and proper diet – I owe to my time spent in the weight room during my tenure as a member of the Boston College Men's Basketball team.

Chapter XX

Home Games

"Letting go doesn't mean giving up,
but rather accepting that there are things that cannot be."

- Unknown Author

November 10th, the day of our first game against New Hampshire, had finally arrived, and with it, came a truly intense excitement for me and a palpably electric buzz in the locker room. A nervous exhilaration bounced off the walls as we all rolled into Conte Forum one by one, everyone anxiously counting down the minutes until tip-off. For almost half of our young team, this was our first collegiate basketball game, and for the upperclassmen, this was the dawning of their time of leadership – their chance to take a young, inexperienced team from which no one expected much, and make them a viable contender for the NCAA national tournament come mid-March.

On home game days, we would have to arrive at Conte Forum 90 minutes before game time. Naturally, there is a much-heightened security presence at Conte on game days, security guards stationed at each entrance to the arena, preventing people from entering through side doors without tickets. Unfortunately for me, there was also a guard stationed at the side door where players entered the arena. The day of the first home game against New Hampshire, I was walking into the arena with freshman center Josh Southern. When we came to the security table, Josh walked right past the guard, but when I attempted to follow him, the man stopped me and asked for my I.D. When I presented him with my driver's license, he cross-referenced it with what appeared to be a team roster. However, to my dismay, the roster he had was an old copy – a copy without my name present on it. Josh tried to vouch for me, but the young security guard wouldn't permit me admittance into the arena. Despite the fact that I was wearing a Boston College Basketball sweatshirt and sweatpants, the guard said if my name wasn't on the roster, he couldn't let me pass. Thankfully, I had walked in with Josh because he walked upstairs to the locker room and got Coach Cassara to come downstairs and explain to the guard that his copy of the roster was out-dated and that I was, in fact, the walk-on. Not surprisingly, I was stopped and I.D.'d for the first six home games (eventually, the security company, Team Ops, began stationing the same woman at the player entrance and she began to recognize me after a few games).

After gaining admittance into the arena – which clearly proved to be a difficulty on some occasions – I would proceed up to the locker room where I would find my uniform and shooting shirt hanging in my locker. I'm a rather prompt person and thus, would typically be one of the first players to arrive for games; however, on top of simply preferring to be early, I would usually arrive early strategically because if I were one of the first guys to arrive, I'd be one of the first dressed, and consequently, one of the first out onto the court to put up some shots before warm-ups. As soon as the rest of my teammates showed up on the court, it would mean that I would have to stop shooting and focus primarily on rebounding for them. After all, we had 20 team basketballs – our team got 10 and the other team warming up got 10 – and since our team had 13 players, that meant I didn't get a ball to shoot with. Simple mathematics. Furthermore, on the rare instances I would be fortunate enough to get a few shots, what did it actually matter? Why did I even need to warm up? Every shot I took was simply a shot I was preventing one of my teammates from taking and subsequently, another instance I was preventing one of them from getting fully prepared for the game. Please allow me to clarify that this is not me just being negative, but rather, this is me simply being realistic. Warm-ups and pre-warm-ups shoot-arounds are for the guys who play to get loose for the game.

For the first few games, I took this extremely personally. It insulted me that I was not allowed to shoot (I found out later in the season that one of the coaches actually told the scholarship guys to take the ball if I were shooting). I rationalized that if I were, in fact, part of the team, I should be allowed to shoot with the team. Though the more I thought about my situation, the more I realized that it was for the betterment of the team if I just rebounded for Tyrese of Rakim or someone. I finally made peace with the situation when I thought about my high school career when I was the best player on the team and thought about the times I would get frustrated when guys who never played took my shots during warm-ups. Consequently, I came to the realization that while it may be difficult for me to admit, I was not the focal point of this team and thus, had to accept my role on the team – and I did.

As I mentioned, because I couldn't put up any shots when my teammates got onto the court, I would make a concerted effort to get dressed and out onto the floor about 75 minutes before game time. This way, I could put up about 20 minutes worth of shots without anyone else on the court with me (except for Tyler Roche, who was the only player on our team who would get to the arena before me). After about 20 minutes of shooting and working up a light sweat by myself, the rest of the team would make its way down to the court. At that time, I would go over to the weight room and get a full stretch and a Powerade from Nick. Typically, a long line would form to get stretched about an hour before the game, so naturally, following suit with my "arrive early" theory, I would try my hardest to beat the line in the weight room, as well.

Following my stretch, I would proceed over to the training room (a room where players can get taped, get ice for injuries, heat sore muscles, or work on physical therapy routines before or after practices and games) where I would heat and get electric muscle stimulation on my shoulder (an injury I suffered early in the year). The heat and muscle stimulation would usually serve to loosen up my shoulder and take some of the pain away for the game.

At about the 45-minute mark, the entire team would head back up to the locker room where one of our assistant coaches would review the other team's personnel and primary offensive and out-of-bounds sets, somewhat of a refresher course of what we reviewed all week in film sessions and scout team. (There were digital clocks all over the arena – in the weight room, training room, and locker room, as well as the scoreboard on the court – counting down the time remaining until tip-off.) Toward the end of the year, Coach Skinner began quizzing the starters and role players on their match-ups and significant player strengths and weaknesses. I remember sitting in the back of the locker room, like I always did, trying to blend in more than normal (as if I could ever blend in on that team!). I remember being nervous that Coach would call on me when he asked his quiz questions, because as one might imagine, I often had a difficult time paying attention during film sessions. The straightforward truth is that it is almost fruitless to pay attention when there is almost 100% certainty that I will not play, and moreover, if I were to play, it certainly wouldn't be meaningful minutes and would certainly not be against the players we reviewed during film. Fortunately for me, however, Coach Skinner never called on me one time the whole year.

After Coach Duquette, Cassara, or Colson finished his scout review, we would head back down to the court. Before we'd run onto the court, we would group up in a huddle in the hallway leading out to the court. Tyrese and John, the team captains, would give us an inspirational speech or some words of wisdom and then Josh would say a prayer on behalf of the team. When our huddle broke, we would wait in the hallway until we got the "thumbs up" from the security guard monitoring the doorway to the court and we'd run onto the court to the Dropkick Murphys' song "Shipping up to Boston" and begin warm-ups. Warm-ups consisted of a few minutes of lay-up lines, three-man-weave, and finally, a team shoot-around where I would rebound for the rest of the guys.

My favorite part of warm-ups was three-man-weave. However, I would always be sure to stay in the middle line because one of the side lines had to throw an alley-oop and the other side line had to catch the lob and dunk the ball. During the first set of warm-ups of the season, the day of the New Hampshire game, when it was my turn to throw the alley-oop to Corey Raji, I literally threw the ball a foot and a half over the rim, he was unable to catch it, and it slammed off the backboard. Without much surprise, the failed alley-oop was followed by a resounding "Damn Brandon!" from the rest of the guys. Needless to say, that was the last attempted lob pass of my collegiate basketball career.

From the first game on, I made sure I always lined up in the center line during weave.

Another thing I liked to do – more a contest with myself – was to keep track of how many three-pointers I made and missed in warm-ups and then calculate the percentage. One game, on the road against Duke, I made 17 out of 20 three-point shots, shooting a blistering 85% during warm-ups. I joked with my friends and family that I shot 85% against the Blue Devils.

For the last few minutes of warm-ups, the team would put up some shots and I would rebound for them, along with the team managers.

Following the shooting, at the 12-minute mark, the team would once again proceed up to the locker room, where Coach Skinner would be waiting to address us. He would go over a few keys to the game and some focal points, as well as some goals we needed to achieve in order to have the greatest chance at success. For instance, he might say that we needed to win the battle on the glass and out-rebound the other team in order to have a shot at winning. Or he might say that we had to hold the other team under a 40% field goal percentage. Etc.

Following Coach Skinner's pre-game speech, we would return to the court for player introductions and the national anthem. During player introductions I would stand in one of the lines of reserves, flanking the starting five, and as each starter's name was called, he would run through the "gauntlet" of the rest of us, slapping everyone's hands. When all of the starters had been introduced, we would "bring it up" as a team, everyone reaching his hand as high as he could, huddling around the foul line in front of our bench. Typically, during this huddle, music would be blasting, the PA announcer would be talking, and/or fans would be screaming, so it was often quite difficult to hear any of what Tyrese was saying to the rest of the guys. On top of the noise around us, I would often be on the outside of the huddle, behind some of my tall teammates, making it even more impossible to hear Tyrese.

After player introductions was the national anthem. While the Star Spangled Banner was being sung, I would take that time to locate my parents, girlfriend, and friends in the stands. Usually, my parents and Sarah sat directly across from the opposing team's bench, in the hockey penalty box, one row up from the court. Each player on the team got four tickets to give out to family and friends for each home game and we could get more tickets if one of our teammates wasn't using his and was willing to give them up. We had to register our guests on a website called playerguest.com or they wouldn't be able to get into the arena. Once our guests were registered online, they had to go to a specific ticket box at Conte Forum and wait in line with the other players' guests. Usually my mother, father, and girlfriend would be some of the first player guests to arrive, along with the Roche family and the Oates family, so they would get the premium seats in the hockey penalty box.

After the national anthem, Coach Skinner would address the starting five and go over the play for the opening tap and give his last words of advice to the team. Again, I would almost always be at the back of this team huddle and thus, would almost never be able to hear Coach Skinner speak. During these huddles (the same huddles would form during time-outs), I would often people watch, gazing over the thousands of fans, trying to find any of my classmates or anyone else I might recognize in the stands. On the day of the New Hampshire game, I was astounded to see a little boy sitting along the baseline under the far basket wearing a number 10 Boston College jersey. As the season wore on, I noticed more and more number 10 jerseys in the crowds (though nowhere near the amount of number 4, Tyrese; 1, Craig Smith; or 3, Jared Dudley jerseys). Actually, Marshalls Department Store still carries the number 10 jersey (at least they did the last time I was there).

*****

As the New Hampshire game approached the final buzzer with us leading by 10 points, I began to hear a small group of kids behind me yelling, "Put in Bennett! Put in the walk-on!" Of course, with us only holding a 10-point lead, I wasn't put in the game; however, later that night, when I was checking my Facebook messages, I found a message from a kid named Gabi Remz, one of the kids who was yelling, saying that he and his friends were my fan club. In his message he said, "Hey Brennan, great game tonight! You may have noticed there were 3 people cheering for you to get in the game, and that was my father, cousin, and me. We hope we did not embarrass you in any way, and in fact, we hope you like it. We do it because we know you work very hard in practice and we just think you should get to play."

I cannot stress enough how thankful I was for Gabi and the rest of the "fan club." It becomes quite difficult for a player who never plays – and has no real hope to ever play – to remain positive and keep smiling, but when people, like those kids and their father, show that kind of support, it really makes the situation a lot less bleak. Thank you from the bottom of my heart.

After the game, we would go back up to the locker room where Coach would address us one more time and we would get pizza, subs, and soda. I usually never showered after games because I never sweated much and thus, would be one of the first people out of the locker room. Our guests would be allowed to stand about 500 feet down the hallway from the locker room, along the Conte Forum concourse, but often times, kids were allowed to wait right outside the locker room door for player autographs. Almost every time I exited the locker room, I was swarmed by the group of kids. Unfortunately, these kids were usually not swarming me with requests for my John Hancock, but rather, with questions about when Tyrese would be out to sign autographs for them. Every now and then a kid would recognize me and ask for my signature on his or her BC Basketball program or someone would ask for a picture with me, and naturally, I was always extremely happy to oblige. I remember one particular kid, the son of one of my father's friends, asked me if I could sign his hat. I did, but instead of giving it back to him, I went back into the locker room and had all of the guys on the team sign it, too. I always loved signing autographs for kids because despite the fact that mine meant almost nothing, it always seemed to make people happy and that always made me happy.

Chapter XXI

Road Games

"We are all faced with a series of great opportunities
brilliantly disguised as impossible situations."

- Charles Swindoll

Road games at Boston College were certainly unlike any road games I had had at any other point in my basketball career. In high school, we would board a bus and travel no more than 30 minutes to our farthest away games; however, at Boston College, road games could take us as far west as Ann Arbor, Michigan or as far south as Miami, Florida. Traveling for me was always a double-edged sword, meaning there was a great deal I loved about it, but at the same time, much I really disliked. For example, traveling for road games meant that we would get to see many different parts of the country, get to play in some of the most famous arenas in college basketball, stay in fancy hotels, and often miss an entire day of classes – sometimes even being fortunate enough to miss a test or a quiz. However, the flip side to that is that sometimes we would have games on weekends and I wouldn't get to see Sarah that week, I would miss a class where attendance counted very highly toward the overall grade and the teacher would only allow so many absences, or, as the season wore on, I would have to travel 2,000 miles and for two days without having any hope of playing at all.

I remember early in the season, before we even played our first game, John Oates, Tyler Roche, Joe Trapani, and I were all sitting in the locker room before practice and I asked them what we do for road games. I asked if we drive or if we fly or if we do both depending on the distance. Joe started laughing and Tyler shook his head. Oates looked at me and laughed, saying, "Man, we would fly to the Boston Garden. This is Division 1." While he was obviously being sarcastic, and we actually did drive to the Garden, we flew to every other away game.

For a normal road game, we would leave the morning of the day before the game. For example, if we had a game on Thursday night at 7 p.m., we might leave on Wednesday morning at 9 a.m. Typically, we would fly out of Logan International Airport in Boston, or occasionally we would fly out of Bedford-Hanscom Field Airport, a much smaller airport in Bedford, Massachusetts. Most of the time, we would fly commercial out of Logan on the way to the game, but we would have a charter flight back to Boston. Occasionally, we would fly commercial both ways, and very rarely, we'd have two charter flights. On trips that we would travel commercial, we had to wear dress pants and nice shoes, which was far less comfortable than wearing a sweat suit when we flew charter. Furthermore, we almost always had to sit in coach seating on the plane, while Coach Skinner usually sat in first class (I guess that's one of the perks that comes with being a Division I basketball coach). Though, I must admit, flying charter wasn't always very comfortable either. Charter planes were typically very small, which meant that there wasn't a whole lot of room for some of the bigger guys on the team. On the charter planes, there were two rows of seats – one row had two seats and on the other side of the aisle, the other row only had one seat. Because I was one of the smallest guys on the team – and on the plane for that matter – I always had to sit on the side of the plane with two seats, and moreover, I always had to sit with one of the biggest guys on the team, like Tyrelle or Josh, which needless to say, made for a rather cramped flight.

Before we got to the airport, while we were on the bus, one of the team managers would pass out an envelop to all of the players, containing the trip's meal money and a laminated copy of the trip's schedule. Typically, we would get about $50 for meal money, but depending on the length of the trip and the distance away, we might get more or less. For instance, the night we played Providence at the Boston Garden, we didn't get any meal money, because we went back to school that night; however, during the ACC tournament in Charlotte, North Carolina, we got $65 and because we won a game and had to stay an extra day, we received another $20.

I loved the fact that we got so much meal money, especially because of the fact that we really didn't need that much. We usually had a free meal right when we got to the hotel at which we were staying, we always got free breakfast the morning of the game, and we always got a pre-game meal on the day of the game. That means that we literally only had to pay for one meal ourselves – dinner after practice on the night before game day. What I would do is just go with Oates, Roche, and Daye Kaba to McDonald's or Subway for dinner and pocket the remaining 40 or 50 dollars. Sometimes, I would even bring a couple of pre-made sandwiches from the BC dining hall and just save all of my meal money – something that John always made fun of me for, saying that I was cheap. I remember telling one of my good friends and high school teammates, Mike Perreault, who plays Division III ball at MCLA, about how much money we got for meal money and he was just astonished. He informed me that he only gets $7 per game.

The other object in the envelop was an itinerary which listed all the events we would do while on the trip and their expected times. For example, the schedule might read:

Wednesday:

9:00 a.m. – Depart BC for Logan International Airport

10:00 a.m. – Arrive at Logan International Airport

12:00 p.m. – Flight leaves for Raleigh-Durham
                     International Airport

3:00 p.m. – Arrive at Raleigh-Durham International Airport

5:00 p.m. – Check into Marriot Hotel

5:30 p.m. – Dinner in hotel dining hall

7:00 p.m. – Depart for practice at Smith Center,
                     University of North Carolina

9:00 p.m. – Return to hotel

11:00 p.m. – Room checks

11:30 p.m. – Lights out

Thursday:

9:00 a.m. – Breakfast in hotel dining hall

10:00 a.m. – Depart for practice at Smith Center,
                     University of North Carolina

12:00 p.m. – Return to hotel

2:30 p.m. – Film in hotel conference room A

3:00 p.m. – Pre-game meal in hotel conference room B

5:00 p.m. – Depart for game

7:00 p.m. – **Beat UNC**

10:00 p.m. – Depart for Raleigh-Durham International Airport

1:00 a.m. – Arrive at Bedford-Hanscom Field Airport

2:00 a.m. – Arrive at BC

One of my favorite parts of traveling was staying in the different hotels across the country. My roommate on every road trip was John Oates. I was so nervous that I would be stuck with one of the guys who didn't really like me or one of the guys who picked on me the most; however, I was relieved to learn that I would be rooming with John all year. My favorite part about rooming with John was the fact that he liked most of the same things I liked – namely, sleeping. If you look over the sample schedule, you might notice that while we are relatively busy with practices and film sessions, there is still a lot of free time worked into the itinerary. In our room, almost all of this free time was devoted to napping. On the rare occasions that we weren't catching some afternoon z's, we would watch television or I would play old Sega Genesis and Super Nintendo games on my laptop. Sometimes after the night practice on the days before games, Oates, Roche, and I might hit the pool, hot tub, or sauna to relax a bit. Quite frankly, whatever we were doing – eating, sleeping, watching TV, hanging out in the pool, or relaxing in the sauna – was far more fun than sitting in a classroom or taking a test.

*****

Another one of my favorite aspects of traveling across the country for road games was the fact that I got to play – well, warm up – in some of the most amazing college basketball environments in the country.

The first ACC road game we played was at the University of Maryland. For each road game, we got a minimum of two guest tickets; however, for some of the larger venues, we would get upwards of six tickets each. Unfortunately, because I never played, and the likelihood of me getting into a game when we were up 30 points (Coach Skinner never put me in the game when we were down a significant amount of points) was very slim, my parents never came to any of the away games. The positive side of that, though, was that each time we played at a school near the home state of one of my teammates, I was able to give him my tickets so he could have some extra guests come to the game.

During our first ACC road game against Maryland, I was very excited to experience what an ACC game was like in another team's arena. I was forewarned that the atmosphere would be very hostile and extremely energetic, but truthfully, I was looking forward to a really loud, high-energy game. Because not much was expected from us during the 2007-2008 campaign, we didn't always have sell-outs during home games, and subsequently, Conte Forum never got very loud. On the contrary, Maryland was arguably the loudest place we played all year (N.C. State was also incredibly loud), seating almost 18,000 people in the Comcast Center. For the Maryland game, I wore my uniform to the arena under my sweat suit so I could be one of the first players out onto the court to get up some shots, but when I went out to shoot, none of my teammates warned me that I should wear a shooting shirt over my jersey. Without this word of warning, I walked out onto the court wearing just my jersey, exposing my identity to the crowd (most of the student section had already arrived). I heard some of the harshest insults I'd ever heard at Maryland while I was shooting – comments ranging from killing my family to breaking my legs.

*****

One of my favorite places that we played was Cameron Indoor Stadium in Durham, North Carolina, the home of the Duke Blue Devils. The first thing I noticed when I walked into Cameron Indoor for the first time was how exceptionally small it is, capable of holding just over 9,000 people. The stands seem to come right out onto the court, which obviously gives Duke a tremendous home-court advantage. If you've ever watched a Duke Basketball game on TV, you can see how the stands' close proximity to the court affects the game. During dead balls, when the opposing team is inbounding the ball on the opposite side of the court, in front of the student section, all of the students near the inbounder lean toward the ball and reach their hands out as far as they can, almost touching the opposing player.

Cameron Indoor is an incredible basketball atmosphere, both loud and electric with energy; however, when you're a visitor in Durham, it certainly isn't a welcoming place to be a basketball player. Without a doubt, the fans at Duke were by far the most hostile towards us. (If there are any Dukies reading this book, you are definitely the best fans in the ACC, and perhaps the country.) From the second I ran onto the court – the way onto the court is a narrow strip of floor leading us right through two flanks of Duke fans – the fans began hassling me and screaming out insults. *"You aren't going to play tonight, white boy!" "You better get comfortable on that bench; it's going to be a long night!"* Of course, there were also the more profane insults that I will omit from this narrative for the reader's sake.

Usually during road games we would come out to the court and shoot, the same way we did at home, but because I couldn't get to the gym any earlier than anyone else, I was unable to get out to the court before everyone and get shots up. Unfortunately, this meant that I was unable to shoot, so I would focus on rebounding. Usually, Tyler would ask me to give him a stretch, so we would go near half court and I would give him a quick stretch. We would almost always stretch before road games and the crowds would typically ignore us – usually because the students from whatever school we were playing at hadn't arrived yet. This was certainly not the case at Duke.

At Duke, the entire student section was present and jumping up and down from the moment our team walked into the arena until the game was over. Furthermore, at the sight of me stretching Roche, all of the fans began chanting in unison, "1, 2, 3, 4, 5, 6, 7, 8, 9, 10, swwwiiiiiiiitch it up!" and then they would throw their hands up in a lasso motion before beginning the count again. It almost becomes hard not to laugh out loud, because truthfully, some of the chants and cheers they do are pretty funny. One of my favorites they were yelling was, "Oates for breakfast, Rice for lunch! Oates for breakfast, Rice for lunch!"

After I finished stretching Roche, some of the guys went back into the locker room, which meant that I could shoot for a while. Locker rooms on the road were, needless to say, nothing like the palace of a locker room we had back at Conte. Rather, these locker rooms, especially the one at Duke, were a bit more like the ones we had back in high school – cement floors, metal chairs (if they gave us chairs), rusty lockers, and very confined quarters. Some were a bit nicer, perhaps having carpeted floors, but again, nothing compared to being in our home locker room. Anyway, as I mentioned, after I finished stretching Roche and the Duke student section caught its collective breath, some of my teammates headed back for the locker room and in doing so, allowed me to shoot for a while. As I mentioned last chapter, I literally shot the lights out in warm-ups at Duke, making almost every three-pointer I took. Surprisingly, the more I shot, the less the fans kept yelling insults, but rather, they began to cheer every time one of my shots tickled the twine. It doesn't take a 3.9 GPA to realize that these cheers were completely in mockery; however, hearing cheers is a bit easier on the psyche than hearing jeers (regardless if the cheers are, in fact, jeers!). After I had hoisted 15 shots or so, the rest of my teammates began to come back out. After I made a three-pointer, Rakim Sanders took my ball instead of passing it back out to me. Upon the theft, the crowd began to rain boo's down upon him, yelling, "Hey, give the white kid back the ball!" "Let the little one shoot!" On top of telling people that I shot 85% from "three" against Duke, I was also able to say that the most hostile fans in college basketball actually cheered for me, though I never mentioned that the threes were in warm-ups and the cheering was simple mockery!

Interestingly enough, however, my most memorable moment of playing against Duke had nothing to do with basketball. Instead, what I'll remember most was getting the chance to shake hands with Coach Krzyzewski after the game. I've always admired "Coach K" and his coaching style so getting to shake his hand was truly an honor.

*****

Another exciting venue I was fortunate enough to play at was the Smith Center at the University of North Carolina at Chapel Hill.

Contrary to the arena of their Tobacco Road rival, Duke, UNC's Smith Center was enormous, having a seating capacity of more than 21,000! Also unlike Cameron Indoor, the seats at the Smith Center were back off the court a little, making it a bit easier to breath in the arena. However, what UNC fans lack in proximity to the court, the certainly make up for in number and volume. Literally, all 21,000+ UNC fans are wearing powder blue and each and every one of them bleeds for their team. Needless to say, UNC is a tough place to play basketball (as if playing against UNC wasn't already tough enough).

One of the most breathtaking aspects of the Smith Center, however, is the sight of all of the retired jerseys hanging from the rafters. It is amazing to think that all of those NCAA and NBA greats once played on the same court on which I was standing. After our night-before-the-game practice, I took out my cell phone and snapped a few pictures of some of the jerseys – Rasheed Wallace, James Worthy, Phil Ford, and of course, Michael Jordan, just to name a few.

*****

My absolute favorite place at which we played a road game during my time at Boston College was, ironically enough, the closest place to home – the TD Garden. Early in the season we played Providence College at the Garden in The Hartford Hall of Fame Showcase game, and despite losing 98-89 in overtime, the experience was truly amazing. I remember standing on the famous parquet floor during warm-ups, absolutely in awe that I was playing basketball on the same floor that the World Champion Boston Celtics play on (I always joked that my presence on that court must have been the reason why the Celts went on to win their first NBA championship in 22 years.). I remember looking up into the rafters and seeing all of the banners for the Celtics' 16 NBA championships as well as all of the retired Celtics' greats' jerseys and just feeling like a kid in a candy store. I wanted to take pictures and capture that moment forever.

Another awesome thing about warming up on the parquet was that the NBA three-point line was still visible on the floor so each time I happened to get a ball during shoot-around, I would launch a three from NBA-range. It's hard to grasp how deep an NBA three-pointer really is until you shoot from the actual line. I felt like I almost threw the ball more than shot it.

After the game, when we got back to the locker room, there was a The Hartford Hall of Fame Showcase backpack waiting in each player's locker. In the backpack were a Nike watch and a pair of Nike sunglasses. As if getting the privilege of sitting on the bench at the TD Garden wasn't enough, we got gifts for playing in the game, too.

One other unique aspect of playing and practicing at the TD Garden - something I often brag about to my friends, but never mention around my girlfriend - is that we got to see the Celtics dancers up close and personal. I remember the day before we played Providence, during practice, I had to go to the bathroom so I walked off the court and turned down a hallway. As I walked around the arena looking for a bathroom, I walked right through the Celtics dancers practicing, and actually asked one of them where I could find a bathroom.

Traveling with Boston College Basketball proved to be a very unique and altogether enjoyable experience, although, as the year progressed and my enthusiasm for my situation began to dwindle, traveling became more of an inconvenience than a privilege.

Chapter XXII

Meeting Carl Beane

"Ladies and gentlemen, boys and girls, welcome to Fenway Park."

- Sherm Feller / Carl Beane

One thing that anyone who knows me understands is that I am a diehard Red Sox fan (as I've mentioned a few times). I watch as many games on TV each summer as humanly possible and I try to get to Fenway as often as my bank account will permit. One can imagine my excitement when midway through the 2007-2008 basketball season, I had the enlightening experience of meeting Carl Beane, the voice of the Red Sox (the guy that says, "Now batting, David Ortiz!" in that booming, sends-chills-racing-up-and-down-your-spine-because-you're-actually-at-Fenway-Park way).

As my teammates and I finished up our usual pre-game routine – lay-ups, weave, and shoot-around – I caught sight of my father and Sarah in the stands speaking with a man whom I did not recognize. Furthermore, I noticed the odd levity of their conversation, as all three seemed to have caught a case of "the smiles." Before I returned my attention to Coach Skinner and the game at hand, I watched this man hand what appeared to be his ring to Sarah, and subsequently, I watched her slip it onto her ring finger.

After the game, when I finished changing and left the locker room to meet my family, Sarah was elated to explain to me the strange happenings I had observed a few hours earlier in the stands. She explained to me how the man she and my father were speaking with was none other than Carl Beane and furthermore, her elation quickly blossomed into total euphoria as she showed me pictures of her wearing Mr. Beane's 2007 Red Sox World Series Championship ring. Needless to say, I was in a state of complete awe, and moreover, quite jealous toward Sarah's good fortune.

What surprised me more, however, was that at the moment when Sarah could obviously sense the green-eyed monster erupting from inside of me, she produced from her pocket one of Mr. Beane's business cards, which displayed his email address. She informed me that he requested that I email him because he wanted to meet me. (Apparently, my father had told him that I was interested in a career in broadcast, which, at the time, I was absolutely interested in.)

When I returned to my dorm that night, I quickly sent out an email to Mr. Beane, first thanking him for his benevolence toward my family and girlfriend, but moreover, his willingness to reach out to me and request a face-to-face meeting. I told him that I'd gladly meet with him as soon as possible. I was delighted to receive a response email from him quite promptly, and we subsequently scheduled a meeting.

A few days later, I had the privilege of speaking directly with Mr. Beane and his charming wife (and I had the chance to see his ring in person, too!). I was initially amazed to hear his voice in person because he sounds exactly the same as he does over the loudspeaker at Fenway Park. Mr. Beane and I talked for about half an hour about his career, how he got his start, and the steps I would need to take to begin a career in broadcasting. As if I were not impressed enough with his character, as we parted ways, Mr. Beane told me that if I ever do pursue broadcasting as a career and I ever created any broadcast that I wanted him to take a look at or listen to, he would be more than willing to do so. To this day I still email Mr. Beane to check in every once in a while and had it not been for my involvement with the Boston College Basketball program, I may never have had this tremendous experience.

Chapter XXIII

The Down-Side of "Up"

"Nothing is so difficult as not deceiving oneself."

- Ludwig Wittgenstein, *Culture and Value*

Games flew by in a mundane and predictable manner, without me gracing the court even a single time. Over the course of the first few games, I was excited to be a member of the team. It didn't bother me that I wasn't getting any playing time because, after all, I was a member of an elite Division I basketball team. However, as the weeks passed, my once-great enthusiasm began to wane. With each passing game, I longed more and more to be an integral member of the team. I wanted nothing more than to play the game I loved and get out onto the court with the basketball in my hands. The night of January 2nd, when we were to play Longwood University, arrived in much the same way, my fervor for my situation at an all-time low. I expected to leave my seat on the bench only a few times on that night – for each time-out and once at halftime. However, before I address the Longwood game, I feel that it is important that I speak to the reasons why my enthusiasm and zeal were reaching unthinkable lows.

I can only imagine what my reader must be thinking. *How can you be so negative about such an amazing situation? Okay, so you don't get playing time and you don't get to play a whole lot in practice...That isn't so bad.* The simple truth is that it was exceedingly difficult for me to remain positive in mindset when my experience was turning out to be nothing like I had envisioned. As I mentioned before, despite the fact that Preston had offered me the warning that I probably wouldn't play at all, I held firm to the belief that somehow, someway, I would prove to the coaches that I *could* play Division I basketball and that I deserved to be on the court. Unfortunately for me, nothing seemed to be working out in my favor. And despite the fact that I never got the opportunity to play or practice, a number of other aspects of my situation were turning sour.

First and foremost, I was the only non-scholarship player on the roster. I suppose the average person wouldn't understand why this was a problem; however, the fact that I was non-scholarship came with some significant baggage. First, and obviously most importantly, I had to pay for my education. I was fortunate enough to receive some local scholarships and a nice financial aid grant from the university, but despite these grants, I was still paying a very large sum of money each year to attend Boston College. Furthermore, the fact that I was playing basketball - it being a colossal time commitment - meant that I could not afford the time to get a job. Theoretically, if I could have worked a campus job or a local job, I would have been able to make a few thousand dollars over the course of the year and significantly reduced my yearly debt. Obviously, the players on scholarship didn't have to worry about this.

Another negative part of not being a scholarship athlete was the fact that I wasn't privy to a weekly meal called "Training Table." Each week, the 12 scholarship guys would go to Training Table where they would get to eat a free healthy meal that was a part of the diet plan we were supposed to be following. Instead of going to Training Table, I would have to eat in the dining hall, which, like everything else non-scholarship students do, costs money and unlike Training Table, presented the temptation to eat unhealthily.

Yet another negative part of not being on scholarship was that I had to buy my textbooks, which as any student knows, can be quite costly. During my tenure with the BC Basketball team, I was a biology major, and consequently, I was taking mainly science courses, each one requiring a large - and expensive - textbook. I would find myself spending upwards of $500 on books each semester out of my own pocket, where as my teammates would be able to save that money. Furthermore, the college still offered my teammates grants (i.e. Pell Grant) which they obviously didn't need, so literally, these grants turned into spending money for them. Furthermore (I know this is getting redundant), at the end of the semester, when I would sell my used textbooks back to the bookstore for a fraction of what I paid for them, the guys on my team would also be allowed to sell their books back, but for pure profit.

Another aspect of my situation that began to get me down as the season progressed was the fact that it was becoming exceedingly difficult to keep up with my classes. As I mentioned earlier in my narrative, I was the valedictorian of my high school class, and thus, school has always come rather naturally to me. I never had to use the student tutoring center that the college provides its students, nor did I ever have to go to the student-athlete learning center while a member of the team. (Student-athletes at Boston College are required to be in attendance at the student-athlete learning center in the Yawkey Athletic Complex for a certain number of hours each week where they would receive tutoring, other kinds of assistance, or just a quiet place to get homework done. However, I, not being scholarship, was not required to go, though I was still allowed to use the facility if I ever needed anything. Actually, one perk of being on the team was that for my second semester, I had my classes registered for me ahead of time so I was guaranteed to get the classes I wanted. My teammates' class schedules, however, were picked for them and they were assigned certain classes for their majors.) As I was saying, I have never had to do much more than minimal studying to pass classes with high marks. However, as the season wore on and traveling became more and more frequent, I found, for the first time in my life, that I was having a difficult time keeping up with my studies.

As I previously stated, I was a biology major with a pre-med concentration during my sophomore year at BC, which meant that I was taking some pretty difficult classes. I was taking a molecular cell biology course and an organic chemistry course on top of a class in social theory, a philosophy course, and an intermediate Spanish course, and for the first time in my life, I felt like I was in over my head. Throughout my entire schooling career, I had never received a grade lower than an A-; however, during this semester, I felt like I was certainly on my way to a lower GPA.

A few weeks into the season, I got an organic chemistry test back and was startled to learn that I had received a 51/100 on the test, one of the lowest grades in the class. While I knew that I didn't put significant time into studying for this exam, I certainly didn't enter the test ill-prepared. Unfortunately, I knew that I had to make a choice about what was more important to me – basketball or remaining pre-med. The next day, I went to student services, dropped the chemistry course, and changed my major to communications (a major which I kept for a semester and then changed to English with a communications minor), effectively abandoning my one-time dream to be a doctor. I knew that the difficulty in the class would remain because of my lack of time due to basketball and my grade point average would certainly have suffered, making it tremendously difficult to get into medical school in the future.

Looking back on that decision, I certainly do not regret it. I realize that life is about making sacrifices in the pursuit of happiness and at that point in time, I did what I thought was best for me. Either way, that decision would pale in comparison to one that I would make a bit further on down the road.

One final difficulty I was facing was the fact that for a significant portion of the season I was physically hurt. Early in the season I suffered a series of muscle strains which I reluctantly played through and even a slight hamstring pull which luckily didn't leave me sidelined. However, one day in the weight room in the early part of the season, I hurt my shoulder pretty badly during a "max-out" bench press repetition, an injury that would plague me for the rest of the season. The truly unfortunate part was that I knew I couldn't miss practice.

One day very early in the season, I came to practice sick with the flu. After practice commenced, I realized that I wouldn't be able to keep up with the running without getting sick, so I asked to be excused from practice and went to see the head trainer. Upon telling the trainer that I couldn't practice, I was harshly scolded and told that I had to practice. He literally screamed at me, telling me that I should have told him before practice started that I was sick because the team was already depleted (Tyrese, Biko, and one of the big guys were nursing injuries and not practicing) and that without me at practice, Coach Skinner would have to completely alter practice because there would only be nine guys. At that moment, I was struck with a staggering realization. Like a ton of bricks hitting me square on the forehead, I realized one of the major reasons why I was on the team: I was a glorified practice player.

I realized that day, that there were two reasons why I was a member of the basketball squad – one, to bolster the team GPA, and two, to fill in for the scholarship players if they had to miss practice. My mother constantly told me that this was not the case, and that I was on the team because I was a good basketball player; however, I couldn't help but think she was wrong. After all, why couldn't this elite Division I program shell out a little more dough for one more scholarship player? Why wouldn't this program just bring in one more 6' 10" player or one more point guard, even if he was only a Division II or III caliber player? Why would they settle for an unathletic, barely 6' tall kid? Furthermore, why would Coach Murphy ask how my grades were before he offered me a spot on the team? If he were truly impressed with my guts and resolve for playing in that pick-up game every day, why should my grades have mattered at all? And finally, the question that often haunted me throughout the year during the times when I felt the lowest, if my grade point average hadn't been 3.92, would he have been so willing to offer me this roster spot? If instead I had had a 3.0, would I have had to try-out? Would he have even offered me a try-out at all? The next day, I got a cortisone injection in my shoulder and missed practice. I didn't miss a single practice for the rest of the season.

Chapter XXIV

Playing Time

"Everybody pulls for David, nobody roots for Goliath."

- Wilt Chamberlain

Despite the fact that I was becoming quite unhappy with my situation as a member of the Boston College Basketball team, I found that the season was progressing just the same – as inevitably as ever. I wasn't playing and there was simply nothing I could do about it. No matter how well I played in practice, no matter how many players were injured or ineligible, or (on an Al Skinner team) no matter how badly we were losing, I wouldn't ever get a chance to play in a game. I suppose however, "inevitability" is only a word and my saying that my season was "progressing inevitability" is probably a defeatist attitude. I once heard a Martin Luther King, Jr. quote, in which he said, "Change does not roll in on the wheels of inevitability, but comes through continuous struggle..." Nevertheless, I felt as though I had been struggling all year and I was unfortunately not seeing any change.

As I was mentioning, January 2nd, the night of the Longwood game, came at a time in the season when I felt like I was at the lowest point I had been at. However, on that night, my "change" rolled in and my struggles finally paid off.

That night, Coach Skinner spoke in his usual soft-spoken tone. So softly, in fact, that I could not hear a word he said. I stood at the back of the huddle, lost behind the wall of seven-footers, left to wonder what my coach was dictating. I fought the urge to watch the thousands of BC-clad people surrounding me in a sea of maroon and gold, commanding my eyes to return to the white board on which Coach drew up the play for the opening tap. I could barely see the board, catching fleeting glimpses of the black marker through the gaps in my teammates' arms as they swayed nervously to and fro.

The huddle broke and I found my usual seat on the far end of the bench, three seats from the end, next to the head trainer and Joe Trapani, the transfer from Vermont who had to sit out a season (NCAA Division I transfer rule). I took my seat and, for the first time, noticed how cold the arena was. The light perspiration I had built up in warm-ups quickly became a cold sweat as currents of cool, winter air rushed over the court, chilling me as I watched the minutes slowly melt from the game clock. My uniform was too big, my shorts constantly slipped from my waist, my shooting shirt was terribly uncomfortable, and my shoes were too small. No nerves created anxious feelings in my mind. No adrenaline coursed through my veins. I was, frankly, a little bored.

The game wore on, my teammates building a substantial lead by halftime, opening up a 17-point margin at the intermission. The second half continued much the same way and as the clock approached the final buzzer, we led by almost 30. With every minute that dissolved off the game clock, I watched another of my fellow reserves enter the game to a roar of cheers. At the five-minute mark, Josh Southern. At four minutes, Daye Kaba. When the clock displayed three minutes remaining, Cortney Dunn checked in.

As the seconds ticked off the clock, I began to shift nervously in my seat. My palms began to sweat. Suddenly, from behind our bench, I heard a choral eruption from a small group of fans. "We want Bennett!" they screamed in unison, clapping their hands each time they paused for another breath. Without warning, the cheer began to spread like wildfire through the arena. Within seconds, hundreds of people were singing pleas for Coach Skinner to put his walk-on into the game. As more and more people adopted the chant, I began to get playful smirks and elbow nudges from my teammates, each of them wanting me to get into the game as much as the fans did. "We want Bennett!" echoed around Conte Forum in stunning musical harmony. I couldn't help but smile wryly each time it sounded. "We want Bennett!"

At the two-and-a-half-minute mark, I unzipped the front of my shooting shirt in preparation for Coach to call my name. I continued to shift in my seat, trying to quickly stretch a game's worth of cold muscles.

"We want Bennett!" All of a sudden, as the time on the game clock dipped below two minutes, Coach Murphy called my name and told me to get into the game. I ripped off my shooting shirt as quickly as I could and ran to the official scorers' table. With 1:46 remaining in the contest, the ball went out of bounds and I was subbed into the game to an explosion of cheers.

As soon as I walked out onto the floor, I noticed how different it felt compared to practice. The floor was incredibly sticky, like fly paper, and springy, too, offering plenty of give with each step. The thousands of fans became one huge blur, casting an aura over the court, showering me in unseen energy, causing an adrenaline explosion in my body. The lights were hot – a stark contrast to the coolness of the bench, allowing my muscles to loosen with unimaginable ease.

When I entered the game, we were on defense. Longwood swung the ball around the perimeter and as they reversed the ball, Daye Kaba jumped the pass, stealing the ball, and led a fast break. Daye took the ball down to the baseline, drawing the defender with him, and as I streaked down the court toward the basket, Daye found me in his peripheral and delivered a perfect pass into my hands. I caught the ball, laid it high off the glass from the left side, and watched it slide poetically through the net for my first, and only, career basket. As the ball went through the net, my teammates jumped and cheered. I ran back on defense, under a deluge of cheers, smiling ear to ear with child-like delight.

The final buzzer sounded a few seconds later and a strange feeling began to wash over me. I felt incredibly jubilant, but at the same time, peculiarly unfulfilled. As I jogged off the court behind my teammates, I caught my father's eyes in the crowd across from our bench where the team guests sat. His smile, broad and bold, showed his pride. He reached out and pulled me close, hugging me as ferociously as ever. "You did it," he said. "You accomplished your goal. You played college basketball!"

As he issued these words of congratulations, I felt that strange feeling consume me once again. I looked around the arena, watching the thousands of departing fans who only moments ago had offered me cheers of pity. I looked at the lights, the baskets, the lines of the floor, and finally, at the uniform I wore. I looked up at my father and all sounds seemed to flee for the exits alongside the maroon and gold wave of fans. I thought of the hours of hard work I'd put in over the last few months. Was it all for *this* moment? I thought of the people singing my praises and of the reporters writing news columns about my *accomplishments*. Did I really accomplish anything? I thought of the time spent standing on the sideline watching practices. Was it all really worth it, or was there more out there for me? Most importantly, however, I thought of the time spent standing on the outside, looking in.

"I need to transfer," I said.

Chapter XXV

Decisions, Decisions

"So close no matter how far. Couldn't be much more from the heart.
Forever trust in who we are, and nothing else matters."

- Metallica, "Nothing Else Matters"

"That would be the first big mistake of your adult life," my mother said to me on the phone after I told her that I needed to transfer.

The days following the Longwood game were probably the toughest of the season for me. The possibilities - schools to consider, basketball programs to research, coaches to get in touch with, or staying put - whirred around in my head, moving in a million different directions, making it extremely difficult to focus on anything else. I started weighing my options and quickly found myself faced with a dilemma. Because I had already tried the transfer process once previously, applying to Division III NESCAC schools - Williams, Middlebury, and Wesleyan - and ultimately turning them down upon my transfer application being accepted, I knew I would most likely not be granted admission another time, even despite the fact that I now had Boston College Basketball on my résumé. This would, therefore, hinder my college search significantly, limiting my Division III possibilities, and possibly only leaving local Division III schools or Divisions I or II to consider.

I instantly ruled out any other Division I schools and while I believe I could certainly play at the Division II level, I didn't want to chance a repeat of my season at BC for some Division II team, and thus, ruled out Division II as well. With my dismissal of DI or DII possibilities, I found myself left with only Division III schools to look at, and as I mentioned earlier, I had already dismissed the NESCAC schools from my search. This therefore, left a few local private DIII options, however, because these schools don't have the tremendous endowment that BC does, yet still cost almost the same price to attend, I was almost forced to rule out these schools – Worcester Polytechnic Institute, Clark, Gordon, etc. – and thus, my dilemma arose. My options, after all my considerations, were A) to remain at Boston College and play basketball for two more seasons, B) to remain at Boston College and not play basketball anymore, or C) to transfer to a Massachusetts state college and play Division III basketball for the next two or three seasons. The question now became whether or not I could give up a Boston College education for that of a small, Massachusetts state college just for the fulfillment of playing college basketball.

A few days after the Longwood game, after I had given myself ample time to digest the possible transfer scenario that was sloshing around in my gut, I called my mother to break the news of my impasse and ask for her opinion on this seemingly non-escapable predicament.

"I'm just not happy here," I told her, "and I think that transferring somewhere might give me some of what I'm missing."

"Well why aren't you happy? And where would you want to transfer to? Would you consider Middlebury or Williams again?" she questioned.

Over the few days between scoring my only career basket against Longwood and my phone conversation with my mother outside of Conte Forum, I had done some significant research into the different Massachusetts state schools and their respective basketball programs. I had ultimately narrowed my choice down to two colleges – Massachusetts College of Liberal Arts (MCLA), formerly known as North Adams State, in North Adams, Massachusetts, or Salem State College, in Salem, Massachusetts. Each school offered its share of benefits, yet each also had its pitfalls.

MCLA offered me the chance to go to a college where I knew I could be an impact player immediately upon arrival. At this point in the 2007-2008 campaign, the Trailblazers were 5-8 and would ultimately finish the season an abysmal 7-18. However, my aforementioned friend and high school teammate, Mike Perreault, was the teams starting shooting guard. Thus, I knew in my head that if Mikey was getting starters' minutes, I would have a good chance to get similar minutes without having to spend significant time or a number of games "earning my place on the team."

Unfortunately, the possibility of transferring to MCLA also had its downside. First, as I said, the basketball team wasn't very talented (record-wise) and judging from the previous season's shortcomings, I decided that this team would not have any serious shot of competing for and capturing a national title. (Cutting down the nets following a national championship victory has been one of my life's dreams for as long as I can remember.) Furthermore, this school is almost a three-hour drive from my house in Central Massachusetts and thus, my family and friends would most likely be unable to see many of my games. What's worse is that I would be almost four hours from my girlfriend, Sarah, who is attending college at – you guessed it! – Salem State.

On the other hand, Salem State College offered me a chance to be on a basketball team that has met with significant success throughout its history. In fact, Salem has won its conference, the Massachusetts State College Athletic Conference (MASCAC) 18 consecutive years, many of those years finishing with deep runs in the Division III national tournament. Furthermore, Salem was losing three senior guards, two of whom were starters on the team, which opened my eyes to the possibility of immediately earning significant playing time. However, the question that presented itself to me was would I play on a team that finished the 2007-2008 season 21-7? Or would I go to Salem and not make the team or not play at all, giving up a Boston College education in the process? Furthermore, I was catching flak from my friends and family, everyone warning me not to go to school with my girlfriend. Everyone assured me that there was no faster way to end a relationship than going to school with your significant other.

"I was thinking about either MCLA or Salem State," I told my mother.

"State schools? Why would you willingly sacrifice a BC education?" she kept asking me, playing devil's advocate. "You're being impulsive and not thinking this through. You're thinking of the immediate future and not the big picture. A Boston College education will give you so many options when you graduate, while graduating from a state school won't offer as much. It is just time to face the fact that your basketball career might never be what it was in high school."

"Well I think that's bullshit. I'm not ready to admit that yet. I can still play and I am going to do it. And besides, an education is what you make of it. There are morons at Boston College and there are very smart people at state schools. If you want something in life, you have to just do it, and it doesn't matter where you go to school."

As I said that, I paused for a second, realizing that that is just it – if you want something in life, you have to go out and get it. I wanted to play basketball again. I wanted to be happy at school. I decided that it was time to go out and make a change.

"You're being impulsive. Think this one through for two seconds."

The truth of the matter was, however, that I *had* thought it through. I had spent the past three or four days contemplating it – weighing my different options and asking myself if transferring was what I truly wanted. Moreover, I had spent the past few months realizing that I wasn't happy and that I *needed* to play basketball again.

As I stood in front of Conte Forum on that sub-freezing January evening, still wet with sweat from practice, I decided once and for all what I must do. I knew I must transfer to a state school to play Division III basketball. I decided that I needed to transfer somewhere where I could actually be a part of a team – a meaningful, important, key-to-the-puzzle part of the team. I needed to go somewhere where I could play Division III basketball and recapture the fire that once burned inside me when the smell of a gym filled my nose. I needed to go somewhere that made the goose bumps line my arms when I thought about hitting the game-winning shot for my new team. I needed somewhere where I could be happy. And in that, the "most rash, ill-advised decision-making moment in my life," I truly was thinking the clearest I could ever hope to think. In that "impetuous and impulsive" moment, I felt like the floodgates opened and into my mind rushed a lifetime's worth of lessons. In that brief moment of clarity in a world full of imperceptions, I believe wholeheartedly that I learned the meaning of my life, something that became even clearer to me in the following months as I proceeded down the winding road of my life's early journey.

*****

The day after I spoke with my mother, while I was on my way to practice, making the lengthy walk from Upper Campus to Lower Campus, I happened to stop into the dining hall to check my mail. When I opened my mail box, I was surprised to find a letter addressed to me, however, what was unusual about this letter was that the address was clearly written in my handwriting.

When I tore open the envelop and removed the contents, I gasped, startled to discover the letter I had written to myself almost a year before at the 48 Hours retreat:

You're
One Step
Closer To
Playing Ball
Again,
Don't Give Up!

I am not an overly religious or spiritual person; however, I couldn't understand how or why this letter would come when it did. Could something like that really be coincident? Perhaps it was just that. Perhaps it was just fortunate timing. Either way, the letter came precisely when it needed to. Had that letter found its way to my mailbox two weeks earlier, I would have crumpled it up and thrown it away, most likely with a bitter taste in my mouth because it reminded me about that retreat. Had the letter come two weeks later, I may have already made up my mind to remain at Boston College and found some rock-solid reason for my decision. Fortunately for me, the letter came precisely at a time when my mind was caught up in indecision, its arrival providing a final shove toward my ultimate decision – transferring. I took the letter as a sign and had there been any small pieces of doubt in my mind after my talk with my mother, there certainly were no doubts anymore. I knew with 100% certainty what I was going to do. The only decision that remained now was where I would transfer to - MCLA or Salem State.

Chapter XXVI

Winter Break

"Life's not fair; get used to it."

- Charles J. Sykes, *50 Rules Kids Won't Learn in School*

During my freshman year at Boston College, when finals ended in late December, I was fortunate enough to have almost five rest-filled weeks of winter break, as classes did not resume until late January. However, during my sophomore year as a member of the basketball team, I did not have this break to rest, relax, and spend time with Sarah and my other friends. Instead, I had to remain at BC, practicing every day, sitting on the bench on game days, and sometimes, even having to travel across the country for days at a time.

As the days of the first semester were winding down, approaching the end of final exams, I was outraged to learn that my entire dorm building would be closing for the winter break. This, unfortunately for me, meant that I had nowhere to live over the break, and the thought of driving an hour on the Mass. Pike each way made me a bit queasy. I did learn that two dorms on campus would be remaining open, the two large dorms on Lower Campus – Vanderslice and Edmunds. I knew that John and Tyler lived in Edmunds, and naturally, I decided to ask them if I could crash at their apartment for the five weeks. As it turned out, they had no problem with me living with them and I ended up rooming with Oates, like I did when we traveled. Joe Trapani, who also lived in my building, roomed with us over the break, too.

When I look back at my time at Boston College, I always realize how much I owe to John. He truly was like a big brother to me and while he might not know it, he definitely had a huge impact on my life. When I was the brunt of a joke, he often deflected the ridicule. When I had questions about anything – basketball or otherwise – he was there to give me an answer. When I had no place to stay over the break, he opened his door to me. And when I was more confused than ever – about the choice to transfer – he told me to follow my heart. He taught me a lot about not only basketball, but about college, and most importantly, about life. He taught me how to relax, to breath, to have a good time, and just to enjoy the ride. He reminded me that life is just too short to worry about everything. To this day I am still in touch with John. Without John Oates, the 2007-2008 basketball season may not have been the experience that it was for me and ultimately, I might not be where I am today without John's influence. I simply cannot thank him enough for the impact he has made on my life.

*****

As much as I was looking forward to spending the break with my teammates at BC, I was more *upset* that I was not spending it in the comfort of my own home with my family, friends, and Sarah. I've always been the kind of person who would rather be at home than at school anyway, so when my few weeks to be at home were taken away, I was not altogether overjoyed. Furthermore, I had recently spoken to Mikey, from MCLA, and he had told me that in Division III, games and practices break for the week of finals and there are no games for a two-week stretch, and therefore, there is ample time to go home and spend the holidays and New Year with family. At Boston College, quite the opposite was true. There was literally no break from "the grind," and when I say literally no break, I mean just that. As finals week progressed, we continued practicing, and a few days before Christmas, on December 22nd, we had a scheduled game against Northeastern. Following the game, we were told that we would have the 23rd and 24th off, but we were expected back on campus for practice the night of the 25th at 5 p.m. Allow me to repeat myself – we had practice on Christmas! Sadly, the extent of my winter break at home was two days and Christmas morning.

*****

At the beginning of Christmas break, we were each given $400 for meal money which was to last us the entire four weeks. Like the meal money we got for road games, I planned to pocket most of this money, namely because my parents had supplied me with a significant amount of groceries and Oates', Roche's, and Trap's parents had also made contributions to our food hoard jam-packing the refrigerator and cabinets in the apartment. Furthermore, when we went on the road for away games over the winter break, we were given even more meal money, and again, I certainly wasn't complaining.

One day after practice, shortly after we had returned from "Christmas break," we came back into the locker room to find a note on the large whiteboard at the front of the room saying: SEE COACH MURPHY. When I went into Coach Murphy's office, he had me sign a sheet of paper indicating that I had received my ACC holiday gift and after I signed the paper, Preston gave me a small box. When I left his office and opened the box, I was astounded to discover an ESPN-brand GPS unit. Just for being on an ACC team roster, I had been given a GPS unit! Oates told me that the year before they had received LCD flat-screen televisions with built in DVD players; the year before that they had been give iPods; and the year before that, they each got $150 gift cards to Best Buy. Furthermore, John said that when we play in the ACC tournament at the end of the season, we would get gifts for that, too. In high school, the closest thing we got to a league gift was having the local Channel 3 sports news team come and broadcast our game on local TV.

*****

One other thing we did over the Christmas break was write letters to under-privileged children from inner-city schools, beginning a correspondence that we would continue throughout the remainder of the year. I really enjoyed writing letters to my seven-year-old pen pal, Alem, but I liked getting letters from him even more. He would always tell me how happy he was to be my pen pal and how he couldn't wait to see me at the end of the year. Each year the BC Basketball team has a picnic with their pen pals at the end of the season – a sort of "fun day" where the under-privileged children get to feel really special for the day. The following is one of Alem's letters to me exactly as it was written:

"Dear Brennan, my favorite sport is basketball. I like to play basketball just lik you. I am doing good in secard grade. Your my penpal. I am so happy to see you. I hope I can see you. By Alem"

In each of my letters to Alem I would tell him that there is nothing more important than studying and working hard in school, promising him that if he did all of his homework, and then practiced basketball every day, he might get to play college basketball at BC someday, like me.

In a letter later in the year, I was overjoyed to learn that Alem was really taking what I said to heart. In his letter he said:

"Dear Brennen, I been good. School is going good. I been practice everyday at home wite my brother like you said. I hope I can be a baskitball player like you. I hope to see you. By Alem"

After the basketball season had concluded, I often spent the weekends at home with Sarah, relaxing. Unfortunately, one weekend very late in the semester, I received a phone call from John Oates asking me where I was. When I inquired as to the nature of his question, he informed me that the pen pal picnic had been that afternoon and I was the only player from the team who wasn't there. When I began to panic, John calmed me down, sarcastically telling me that Alem had sat all alone the whole day, crying, because his pen pal didn't care enough to come see him. After I called him a jackass, he told me the truth – that he had spent the day with Alem and his own pen pal, just telling Alem that I was sick and couldn't be there. Though I felt terribly for not being at the picnic with Alem, I was relieved to hear that John had still made the day fun for him. However, I was outraged with the basketball office and coaching staff, as well as the learning resources department (who were the ones who organized the entire pen pal system), for not informing me of the date. Even had they forgotten to tell me in person, the fact that no one called me to tell me the date and time really upset me.

*****

As the winter break progressed, I found myself more and more engrossed in my new college search and more and more consumed by the idea of once again really playing basketball. After I had narrowed my choices down to MCLA and Salem State, I decided that the first order of business would be to contact the coaches of the two respective programs and inform them that I was considering a transfer to their schools.

I sent Coach Morrison, at MCLA, a short email telling him that I was a 6' guard currently playing on the Boston College Varsity Basketball team and that I was looking to be a more integral part of a basketball program and thus, was interested in a transfer to his institution. The next day, I received a reply email from him basically saying that he was obviously interested in having me as a part of his team and that Mikey had already told him a lot about me as a player; however, it was a violation of NCAA rules to be in contact with a prospective player of another program during the basketball season. He told me that he would definitely be in touch following the season.

With Salem State I had the luxury of having Sarah as somewhat of a liaison between Coach Harvey and myself. When I first told Sarah that I had narrowed my choices down to MCLA or Salem State, she was more than happy to go try to speak to Coach for me. To my delight, she went to Coach's office, walked right in, and had a full conversation with him, explaining to him all about my situation at BC and of how I wanted to transfer somewhere where I could be a contributing member of a team.

When I spoke with Sarah that night, during our nightly two-hour phone conversation, she told me that he was extremely kind and welcoming and moreover, that he was very interested in meeting me and getting to know me better. However, like Coach Morrison told me in his short reply email, Coach Harvey told Sarah that he wasn't allowed to speak with me during the season. He told her to have me contact him as soon as my season was over and to also make sure that I had myself "released" from Boston College Athletics via the compliance and eligibility office.

Needless to say, I was overwhelmed with enthusiasm for the way the infant stages of my transfer appeared to be working out. I was encouraged by the fact that, for the first time in two years, I felt wanted and needed by a basketball coach. As the Boston College Basketball season began to wind down, I finally began to feel like all the stars were aligning themselves for me. Isn't it ironic that I felt lucky to be leaving the BC Basketball team and potentially joining that of a small, Division III state school? I finally began to feel like I was headed toward something better, flying away from the Eagles that had made me feel so alone and toward the one thing that could make it all better – happiness.

Chapter XXVII

The Atlantic Coast Conference Tournament

"My shadow's the only one that walks beside me.
My shallow heart's the only thing that's beating.
Sometimes I wish someone out there would find me.
'Til then I walk alone."

- Green Day, "Boulevard of Broken Dreams"

As the 2007-2008 basketball season came to a close, our team "boasted" a rather unimpressive 13-16 overall record, an appalling 4-12 in ACC play - a record that would almost certainly not earn us a bid to the national tournament for March Madness. Truth be told, I was almost relieved that the season was in its final days. After all, as soon as the season's final buzzer sounded, I planned to be on the phone with Coach Harvey from Salem State and Coach Morrison from MCLA, pursuing the transfer that might lead me to the place I wanted to be - an integral member of a college basketball team. However, there was one thing that could keep our season alive, prolonging the misery that had taken hold of me, restraining me from finally officially beginning the transfer process. The only cloud in the bright blue sky that could rain on my parade was the ACC tournament. If somehow we won the ACC tournament, which was unlikely - though possible - as the 11-seed in a tournament with powerhouses like North Carolina and Duke, we would earn an automatic bid to the national tournament.

Our first game of the ACC tournament was scheduled for Thursday, March 13th, against the University of Maryland, a team that we had beaten once already earlier in the season in their home gym, 81-78. Naturally, everyone felt confident that we could win this game - I suppose as confident as a 13-16 team could possibly feel. Like normal, we left for Charlotte, North Carolina, the site of the 2008 ACC tournament, the morning before game day – Wednesday, March 12th. When we arrived in Charlotte, I was delighted to find that the hotel we were staying at was one of the nicest of the year, but what made the stay even more appealing, was the fact that there were so many media personalities and famous school alumni staying in the same hotel as us.

On the day of our game, as we were walking to the bus to leave for our scheduled morning practice, we walked passed Dick Vitale, one of college basketball's most beloved personalities. If you are unfamiliar with Dickie V, he is the broadcaster who always yells, "He's a diaper dandy, baby!" or "It's awesome baby, with a capital A!" As we were walking by him, he was shaking hands with most of the guys, most of who seemed to be in awe at their good fortune. (It's almost funny how as the season wore on, and I watched my teammates transform from regular kids into big-time college athletes, the "awe-factor" stopped affecting them. In other words, as they were more and more exposed to the "bright lights" of stardom, they stopped being amazed by things. For instance, earlier in the season, Jared Dudley, former BC Basketball star and current member of the NBA's Phoenix Suns, came to one of our practices. At the end of practice, he coached one of the teams during the daily 20-minute scrimmage – the team I happened to be on. Naturally, I was in awe at my luck; however, the rest of the guys seemed to act like the encounter was quite commonplace. It was almost gratifying for me to see them actually in awe at the sight of Dickie V.) As I got closer to him, I could hear him saying, "Boston College in the house!" and as I heard these words, I instantly got goose bumps up and down my arms. However, my ecstasy quickly changed to a sudden pain, for as I walked by Mr. Vitale, my hand stretched out to shake his, (and I swear on my life this actually happened) he jabbed me in the stomach! Yes, he punched me in the stomach. Dick Vitale punched me in the stomach. (As one might imagine, my friends got a nice laugh out of that.) To this day I can't figure out what actually happened in our brief encounter. Perhaps he was trying to give me a "pound," where people bump knuckles. Perhaps I just missed his hand and that was the result. Perhaps he was just trying to give me a love tap or something. If the latter is the case, I have to say that Dick Vitale is the strongest man alive and I wouldn't hesitate to make the statement that he, and not Manny Pacquiao, is the most dangerous pound-for-pound man in the world! Truthfully though, I was honored to meet Dickie V, regardless of the brevity and unusual nature of the encounter. He is truly a great ambassador for the game that we both love and furthermore, college basketball might not be where it is today without selfless people like Dick Vitale.

Another interesting person whom I had the privilege of meeting was former BC wide-receiver Gerard Phelan. After our film session the day before our game, as Roche, Oates, Kaba, and I were on our way to Burger King for lunch, Mr. Phelan stopped us as we were exiting the hotel. He began talking to us about the next day's game, giving us advice about how to defeat Maryland. We must have all looked perplexed, because soon after he began talking to us, he got the same puzzled look and asked, "Do you guys know who I am?" We all looked at each other for what seemed like minutes, none of us having the slightest clue who this man was, until finally John uttered, "No, sorry, who are you?" Mr. Phelan laughed and asked, "Do you guys know Doug Flutie?" Naturally, we responded, "Of course." He said, "Are you guys familiar with the famous Hail Mary pass he threw once upon a time?" Again, we all nodded yes. "Who do you think caught that ball?" he questioned. When we all finally realized who he was, we each shook his hand, he offered us his best for the game the next day, talked with us for a few more minutes, and then returned to the party that was being held in the hotel's bar.

*****

On the day of our game against Maryland, we had a morning shoot-around scheduled at the Time Warner Cable Arena, the home of the Charlotte Bobcats, which was to serve as the site of the 2008 ACC tournament. When we got to the arena, I quickly learned that that morning's shoot-around was going to be different than any other game-day morning practice we had had to date – this practice was completely open to the media and general public.

When we got onto the court, another ACC team was practicing. The ACC has very strict rules regarding scheduled practice times for the ACC tournament. We were not allowed to be on the court until the other team was finished practice (each team had a set practice time limit) and furthermore, we were not allowed to touch the balls until the clock read the exact time when our practice time was scheduled to commence. The team that had been practicing before us had ended their practice a little before the scheduled time so naturally, our team went onto the floor to stretch and get loose; however, when one of our players went over to get a ball, the person monitoring the ball rack wouldn't give him a ball (yes, there actually was a person monitoring the ball rack). When our practice finally did get under way, the open setting proved to be a very strange atmosphere in which to practice. Coach couldn't address us the way he might have had there been no media people present, we couldn't prepare for Maryland at all at the risk of revealing specific game strategy (though we usually didn't go over anything specific to the team we were playing that day during morning shoot-arounds), and the amount of people watching practice simply made the setting uncomfortable. I remember consciously making sure that I took closer jump shots so I wouldn't have to risk throwing up an air ball. I even remember being heckled by a fan from an opposing school – during practice.

*****

More than at any other point in the season, I wanted nothing to do with basketball during our time in Charlotte for the ACC tournament. A few weeks before the trip, Sarah had been diagnosed with some cancerous lumps in her throat and thanks to the Bennett Curse (see Chapter X), her surgery date had been set for Wednesday, March 12th. Of course, this fact meant that I would not be able to see her until I returned from the tournament, so though I hate to admit it, I was honestly rooting for us to lose to Maryland so I would be able to get home by Friday and be with her in the hospital. (Coach Skinner usually liked to fly out immediately following our games, as opposed to staying an extra night in the hotel and leaving the next morning – though there were a select few times when we'd stayed the extra night.)

As the game began, my thoughts were obviously nowhere near Charlotte, North Carolina, but rather, were back home in Massachusetts with Sarah. I felt like I was completely detached from the situation, and truthfully, I remember almost none of the finer details of the game. Much to my dismay, we remained close with Maryland during the first half, only trailing by six points at the intermission.

The second half offered much of the same, as the score remained close for almost the whole game, and with only seven minutes remaining in regulation, we led by two points. As the time on the game clock fast approached zeros, I became Maryland's biggest cheerleader, secretly and emotionlessly bursting out with joy each time they scored a bucket, and at the same time, cringing inside each time we answered with a basket of our own, clapping my hands more in anger than in joy, giving off the appearance of a happy team supporter.

The happy team supporter. That phrase had come to epitomize my role on the team as the year came to its close and with the realization of my role, came a more passionate than ever desire to be finished with Boston College Basketball once and for all. I will never forget the exact moment when I realized this sad truth – the moment that finally doused my fire for Boston College. John's parents, who are two of the kindest people I have ever met, had invited me to come with them to this stunning steak house, Sullivan's, for dinner the night before our game against Maryland. Very graciously I obliged and I was treated to a fabulous meal. (During the meal, Mr. Oates actually suggested that I write this book.) However, after dinner, as we were saying goodnight to them, Mrs. Oates hugged John and told him to "go out there tomorrow and make her proud." When she finished with John, she hugged me and said, "Brennan, you go out there tomorrow and cheer your heart out." Unfortunately, however, I could not be the songbird she wanted. The Raven I had become knew nothing but sorrow.

I smiled and said thank you again; however, inside, I felt like my heart had been ripped from my chest, thrown to the ground, and though she didn't know she had done it, trampled repeatedly by Mrs. Oates. I felt deflated and depressed like never before. (I'm almost tempted to liken the "wind knocked out of me" feeling to the way one might feel after a Dickie V right hook to the gut; however, no feeling is ferocious enough to warrant that comparison!) I was, in fact, a glorified cheerleader, and moreover, I wasn't the only one who knew it. More than ever I knew I wanted to transfer. Furthermore, I realized that not only did I need to transfer, but I now knew that this was one reason why I had to write this book – to reveal to people what it's like being the player at the end of the bench – the cheerleader – rather than the player on the court in the spotlight.

As the minutes began to wind down and the seconds slowly melted from the game clock, our lead began to increase. At six minutes, we led by four. At five minutes, our lead had become six. At four minutes, our lead had stretched all the way to double figures, as we led the Terps of Maryland by 10 points. With just under four minutes remaining in the ball game, I thought all hope was lost, and during the under-four-minute media timeout, I said a quick prayer to the basketball gods, pleading with them, for Sarah's sake, to give Maryland one final gasp and let them send us home so I could be with her. The basketball gods, in an almost tangible battle with the Bennett Curse, heard my prayer and gave the Terrapins the heaping gulp of life they needed, but it wouldn't be enough.

With two and a half minutes remaining in the contest, Maryland had cut our lead from 10 to only three points. However, the Bennett Curse slammed the door on the basketball gods and Maryland, as only one minute and 30 seconds later, with just under a minute remaining in the ball game, our lead was back up to nine. As if in some sick joke, the basketball gods showed up one final time, as Maryland somehow pulled back within three with seven seconds to go. Unfortunately for me, we held onto the lead and won the game by three points which meant that we would play the Clemson Tigers in the second round the next day. I was devastated by my team's win (How often does one hear a statement like that?), invisible tears rolling down a face that was masked by smiles and radiance. I wouldn't get to see Sarah until Saturday.

The next day, Clemson wiped the floor with us, destroying us 82-48. Needless to say, I was relieved that the "ride" was over. First and foremost, I finally got to go home and see Sarah and second, the long, difficult season was finally over (with our losing record, we didn't even make the post-season NIT [National Invitation Tournament]).

After the game, when we were on the bus, Coach told us that because the game had been a 9:00 p.m. start, we were not going to be flying out that night, but rather, flying out the next afternoon. The earliest flight available out of Charlotte was 1:00 p.m., which meant after a three hour flight, an hour bus ride back to BC, and the hour car ride home, I wouldn't be able to see Sarah until late Saturday night.

The next morning when we woke up, John and I noticed immediately that the weather conditions did not look optimal for flying. It was raining rather steadily outside and the sky was ominously dark, suggesting a heavy rain to come. When we flipped on the news, we were quite startled to learn that there was a tornado warning in effect in the greater Charlotte area. How often is there a tornado warning in Charlotte? I lived in Wichita, Kansas for a few years early in my childhood and actually witnessed two tornados; however, a tornado in Kansas is nothing short of expected. A tornado in Charlotte, North Carolina on the other hand, occurs just short of never. A few minutes later, Coach Murphy knocked on our door and informed us that our flight had been canceled due to the severe weather alert and told us that we wouldn't be flying out until sometime Sunday afternoon.

I felt like I had swallowed my tongue and my heart had sunk into my stomach. Now, because of the Sunday afternoon flight, I would not be able to see my girlfriend in the hospital until Sunday night. This is the last time I'm going to say it...the Bennett Curse!

The following day, when the weather had slightly cleared up and the sun decided to come out of hibernation for a few minutes and possibly allow us to get the hell out of Charlotte, we boarded the bus for the final time of the year and headed for the airport. We were flying home on a charter plane and thus, we were flying out of a small, private airport. When we arrived at the airport, we went through the small security presence and took our seats in the waiting room. Minutes passed. A half an hour passed. An hour passed. At the hour mark, we began to wonder why we weren't boarding the plane yet. An hour and a half passed. Finally, after almost two hours of waiting, Coach Murphy told us that the plane on which we were flying home hadn't arrived yet. I felt like yelling, "What do you mean the plane isn't here!?! This is an airport! Let's just use a different one!" I viewed every minute that passed as another minute I wasn't going to be able to spend with Sarah.

Finally, after three hours of waiting, the plane arrived at the airport, unfortunately, it was another half an hour before we were on board the little charter plane. Ultimately, our 1:00 p.m. flight was delayed almost four hours, which meant that I wouldn't get back to Central Massachusetts until close to 10:00 p.m. Sunday night. Sadly, I had to call Sarah's mother and tell her that there was simply no way I was going to be able to make it to the hospital, especially with an 8:00 a.m. class the following morning. Unfortunately, because I had no car and no other way of getting home during the week, I had to wait until the following weekend to see my girlfriend. I didn't end up seeing her until the following Friday, when she was already home from the hospital.

*****

Upon arriving back at BC, the feeling of unease that I had been carrying on my shoulders since the beginning of October had finally abated. I felt free from the game and the team that had imprisoned me for the past six months. I knew I was going to transfer and ultimately, the only thing that remained to do was tell the coaching staff of my intentions. I decided to wait a few weeks to tell them of my decision because had I informed them right away, I wouldn't have been able to use the weight room or gym anymore.

A few days later, after I finished a metabolic workout, I walked up to the locker room and saw a familiar message on the white board: SEE COACH MURPHY. I had almost forgotten that John said we were going to get gifts for playing in the ACC tournament. When I walked into Coach's office, he gave me two brown boxes and a brown leather ACC over-the-shoulder bag (which the guys on my team referred to as a "man-purse"). When I opened the boxes, I was delighted to find a Canon digital camera and a digital photo printer with photo paper. I'm not a big picture taker; therefore, I gave the camera and printer to my mother for her birthday (she was overjoyed by the gifts).

A few weeks later, I mustered up the remaining courage I had – whatever I hadn't spent throughout the season dealing with my teammates and the excessive traveling – and walked into Coach Mo Cassara's office to tell him that I was transferring. I decided to tell Coach Cassara because from the beginning of my time with the BC Basketball program, Coach Cassara was always my biggest supporter and closest "friend" on the coaching staff. He is a Central Massachusetts guy, like me, and if I ever needed anything I knew I could usually turn to him for help. However, what he said to me when I told him I was going to transfer would literally knock me off my feet.

Chapter XXVIII

The Truth Hurts

"You're 5 foot nothin', 100 and nothin', and you have
barely a speck of athletic ability. And you hung in there
with the best college football players in the land for 2 years...
In this life, you don't have to prove nothin' to nobody but yourself."

- "Fortune" from "Rudy"

When I began informing my family and friends of my intentions to transfer from Boston College to either MCLA or Salem State, I obviously received a variety of reactions – some positive and some negative; however, most were altogether predictable. It was a select few reactions, like the one from Coach Cassara, that caught me completely off-guard.

Before I walked into Coach Cassara's office, I had been rather unsure of how I was going to tell him that I was transferring. After all, how do you tell someone who has given you the "chance of a lifetime" that you simply don't want it anymore? When I knocked on his door, he shot a quick glance up over his computer screen, told me to come in, and then returned his gaze to his work. I crept into the office, tentatively taking a seat near his desk and waited for him to address me. Again, he slowly dragged his eyes away from his computer and asked, "What's up?"

"Well, Coach, I don't really know how to say this, but I think I am going to transfer for next year," I said sheepishly.

Coach Cassara shot me a puzzled look, followed immediately by an even more puzzling question, "Have you even thought this through?"

Truthfully, I expected to receive Coach's full support behind my decision. I figured he would be delighted that I was so passionate about the game that I was willing to give up a BC education in the pursuit of playing it.

I told him that I had, in fact, thought it through quite thoroughly and that I had been deeply contemplating a transfer for a few months. I explained how I wasn't entirely happy at BC - both because of the school side of the situation and more importantly, the basketball side of things. I told him that while BC Basketball had offered me an incomparable opportunity - one that I certainly would never forget - it didn't provide me with an opportunity to *play* college basketball, which had been a goal of mine since my youth. Furthermore, I made it abundantly clear that I wasn't leaving out of spite or resentment toward the program, but rather, simply because I was pursuing a happiness that still eluded me.

While I nervously dictated my intentions to transfer, Coach sat reclined in his seat with his feet resting casually upon his desktop, listening intently to what I was saying, an expression of confused transfixion contorting his facial features.

"I think you're being a little quick in your decision," he said in my-mother-like fashion. "I think you need to step back and think for a second about what you would be giving up. Where are you thinking about going anyway?" he asked, all the while maintaining a didactic coach-to-player tone of voice.

"I was thinking about MCLA out in Western Mass. or Salem State. Both DIII schools," I said as if he wouldn't have already known that fact.

"See I just think that's a mistake. I mean, if you were thinking of going somewhere like Clark [where he previously coached] or Babson or Tufts I could understand because you wouldn't be losing anything academically. But to leave BC, which is one of the top 30 schools in the country, for a state school is just not right."

As he spoke, I nodded along, pretending like I hadn't already heard the same speech a thousand times from my parents, friends, and relatives; however, what he said next truly rocked me, sending me into a fiery tailspin of anger - an anger that would control me in the subsequent months, spurring me on toward what I always knew as inevitability.

Chapter XXIX

Moving Forward

"If you have built castles in the air, your work need not be lost;
that is where they should be. Now put foundations under them."

- Henry David Thoreau

"If you had told me that you were transferring to Clark, I could tell you
that you'd probably be the 9th or 10th man on that team. You'd probably
get about five to 10 minutes a game and be a non-impactful player."

I recoiled from his words, shocked, almost as if I had been snake-
bitten by an unseen enemy. A wave of anger rushed over me, followed
by bewilderment, and finally, apathy toward his opinion.

"Okay, well, I just wanted to inform you of my decision. I'd like to
thank you for this tremendous opportunity and thank you personally
for the respect you have shown me throughout the season," I said,
triumphantly in my head, though the anger that had consumed me
drowned out much of the triumph in my concluding remarks.

Before I even gave these words a chance to echo in Coach's ears, I
stood up, walked out of his office, and immediately walked up to the
BC compliance office (on the third floor of the athletic complex) to be
officially "released" from BC Athletics. Having been officially released, I
emailed both Coach Morrison and Coach Harvey, requesting a meeting
with each of them to discuss the possibility of my joining his university
in the fall.

*****

A few days later I heard back from Coach Morrison who seemed
delighted to have the chance to finally sit down and speak with me
personally. We decided upon a day early the next week for me to make

the almost four-hour drive up to MCLA, scrimmage with the team, and meet with him.

*****

Whenever I reflect back upon that scrimmage – which was my first experience playing in a game-like environment comprised entirely of Division III players – I always laugh. For some reason, in my mind, I had this glorious vision of me dominating that game in the same manner as I had dominated high school or summer league games. For some reason, I considered myself *above* Division III – as if I'd effortlessly become an All-American and lead any rag-tag bunch to a national championship. Maybe I had this belief because of some sort of self-appointed right; the notion that because I "played" Division I, I could *obviously* play Division III. More likely, however, this notion existed because, quite simply, I underestimated the high level of competition in Division III.

In high school (taking my high school conference, the SWCL East, as an example), there are maybe one or two skilled players on each team. The "next-level" teams – the kind of teams that win league or state championships – might have three or even four of these skilled players. One has to think, then, that of even this pool of more gifted players, only a few of them will move on to the next level and play any kind of college ball. If, for example, this pool of above-average players is comprised of 10 SWCL East players, maybe only one or two of them is good enough even to play Division III ball, while probably none is talented enough to play in Division I. In actuality, of this aforementioned group of maybe 10 players who graduated in my year, I believe only three of us are currently playing college basketball (all Division III), and to my knowledge, only two of us are getting significant minutes. Even if I examine a larger sample size – say, two years ahead of me and two years behind (2004-2008); a sample of probably close to 40 players – I still believe there are no more than 10 players currently playing college basketball, and in fact, only one of those players is playing Division I. Ultimately, by performing some very general math (and mind you, these statistics are simply suppositions), I can conclude that probably only between 30% and 40% of *the most talented* high school players even continue on to play college basketball at any level. Needless to say, the competition and level of play significantly improves from high school to college. Players are bigger, faster, stronger, and far more intelligent. The advantages that many good high school players always held over the competition – a good first step, a quick release on a shot, size, or wits – typically are no longer significant advantages in the college game and many players never adapt to the level of play. It is the players who are able to adapt their game to the surroundings (and obviously the superstars) who are able to excel in college basketball.

With all that said, you might guess that the scrimmage didn't exactly follow the romantic, Hollywood script I had envisioned in my mind. Throughout the two hours or so of basketball, I felt out of shape, ineffective, and "plain old" stupid. I felt like everyone there was "measuring me up" – judging me and forming some ill-conceived opinion of me because I was supposed to be this "big time" Division I transfer who was supposed to come and lead the troops to the Promised Land (or maybe just take them from 7-18 to a MASCAC title) and I hadn't played overly well. What's worse, however, was that I was unable to meet with Coach Morrison because he wasn't able to be at the college that night. He texted my friend, Mikey, and asked him if I wouldn't mind meeting with him the next day. Unfortunately, I had a test that I needed to study for the following day back at BC and I needed to leave early that morning. Looking back, I don't know why, but when I left MCLA, I never called Coach Morrison to let him know I wasn't going to be able to meet with him – I just left. To this day, I feel terrible about the way I handled things with Coach Morrison. I feel like I really burned a bridge by leaving the way I did.

A few days later, I received a phone call from Coach Morrison, who was not surprisingly, upset with me. He told me that I had to make a decision and offered me a sort of ultimatum – come to MCLA and help them win a league championship or go to Salem State where he would be "knocking us off the mountaintop." I knew at that moment that I was going to go to Salem State College.

Shortly after making my decision to attend Salem State in the fall, I took the train up to Salem to play some pick-up with the team and to finalize my decision. We played for a while and truthfully, I played rather well – far better than I played at MCLA, anyway. I knew for sure I'd be a Viking when I walked off the court that day late in the spring of 2008 because for the first time since high school, I had had fun playing basketball. For the first time since the "glory days," as my best friend Andrew (and Springsteen) likes to call them, I had been consumed by the long-ago-lost feeling of ecstasy. I felt that transferring to Salem State College would ultimately lead to my happiness and thus, my completeness of being.

In the spring of 2008, I began the difficult climb to the top of the mountain where I would await MCLA and Coach Morrison. In the 2008-2009 season, MCLA finished with a record of 1-24 and wasn't able to knock us off any mountaintop.

Chapter XXX

The Boston College
Basketball Banquet

"Two roads diverged in a wood, and I, I took the one less traveled by, and that has made all the difference."

- Robert Frost, "The Road Not Taken"

Shortly after my trips to MCLA and Salem State to play ball with the two teams, I was informed that the Boston College Basketball program would be hosting an "end of the year" team banquet at a local hotel convention room – a kind of closing chapter to our season.

As we drove to the banquet in one of the Boston College vans, some of the guys were discussing who would win some of the different achievement honors that the basketball program awards at the end of each season. Some of the awards included a hustle/attitude award and an academic excellence award, among others. Naturally, we all prodded Dan McDermott, our team video coordinator, with questions because we found out that he had some insider's knowledge as to the recipients of the aforementioned awards. Something told me (call me crazy) that I wouldn't be receiving any awards on that night, though I did hold out some hope that I might receive the academic award, considering the fact that my grade point average was 3.83.

Dan proved relatively difficult to crack, the only information he would supply us with was that the winner of the academic award was in the van (about half of the team was in our van and the other half was in the other team van). With some simple deductive reasoning, the guys narrowed down the winner to either Tyler Roche or me, we being the two players with the highest GPAs. Roche was convinced that I would win the award because he knew that the walk-on had won the award for the past few years (apparently, the walk-on before me, Tyler Neville, had won the award for a few consecutive seasons). The more I thought about the award, and the more I listened to Roche's theory, the more I started to believe that I actually might win the honor. After all, as I had convinced myself many months before, the only reason I was on the team at all was because of my grades. My grade point average was so high (in relation to many of my teammates' GPAs) that it actually brought the team GPA up rather significantly.

When we arrived at the banquet and were being seated in the convention room, I was dismayed to learn that I wouldn't be sitting with the team. The banquet hall had round tables, each one seating six people. Unfortunately, being the team's 13th man, I had to sit at a different table from my teammates with the team managers. I really wasn't upset about this apparent misfortune because, in reality, I enjoyed the company of the managers and didn't mind sitting with them. Truthfully, however, I was insulted that they couldn't squeeze in one more chair around one of the tables to allow me to sit with the team. I thought the entire situation was handled rather poorly. What I realized later, however, and what bothers me more than anything, was that it probably never crossed anyone's mind that it was a big deal for me to not sit with the team and moreover, that I would be insulted by the seating situation.

As the evening progressed, each of the coaches came to the lectern at the front of the room and said a few words about the team and the season. After each of the coaches gave his speech, he announced what award he would be giving out, gave a description of what it takes to win the particular award, and then introduced the recipient of the award. When the coaches finally came to the academic award, I became excited because I was convinced that I would receive the honor; however, again to my dismay, I was let down as Tyler Roche's name was called into the microphone. Needless to say, I was happy for Tyler. He is a very smart kid with a G.PA over 3.0. I chalked up my not receiving the award to the fact that I had only been with the team for one season and that Tyler had been there for a few.

After all the awards had been given out, each of the players on the team was called up to the lectern to receive an "action-shot" framed photograph of himself. One by one, each of the guys made his way to the front of the room until 12 of them were standing in a line across the hardwood floor next to the lectern. Suddenly, everyone began to clap, photographs were snapped, and everyone on the team returned to his seat. I was never called up to receive an action-shot photo.

It occurred to me, when I got back to my room later that night and called my parents, that perhaps the reason why I hadn't received any honors at our banquet was because I had, only days before, informed the coaches that I was transferring. I determined that I had quite literally been snubbed by the basketball program, almost as if I had never been a part of the team.

A few days later when I went into the locker room before shooting around, Preston pulled me aside and apologized for the way "things" were handled at the banquet. He told me that he didn't know why I hadn't received a picture (though he made no amends for why I hadn't been awarded the program's academic honor despite my far superior GPA or why I hadn't sat with the team) and told me that he would have my picture for me in a few days (and I did receive it shortly thereafter). I later learned that my father had called Preston and expressed his displeasure with the way I had been treated at the banquet. Had my father never called to complain, I most likely would never have been given my picture, and moreover, no one would have thought twice about it.

The team banquet was an unfortunate way to end an otherwise enriching, truly life-altering experience. However, when I reflect back upon the end of my time at Boston College, I have no regrets. My time spent with the BC Basketball program was an experience that I will always cherish and would never want to trade. I learned an unbelievable amount about basketball, about life, and about the kind of person I am. Through my experiences at BC, I now know that I can overcome any obstacles life may throw at me. I know that I can do anything I set my mind to and also meet with great success at whatever endeavors I choose to pursue. I have been blessed with a tremendous wealth of experiences and stories that most people only dream of having, and while I didn't always realize it during the moment, I made some friendships that I will treasure for the rest of my life. I sincerely thank Boston College and the

BC Basketball program for affording me the opportunity to attend such an incredible educational institution and to be a part of one of the finest basketball programs in the nation. I am a better person for it.

As I walked out of Conte Forum Athletic Complex for the final time, prepared to begin my journey to Salem State, I was reminded of Robert Frost's words: *I took the one less traveled by, and that has made all the difference.* I hoped he was right.

PART II: SALEM STATE COLLEGE

"A little voice inside my head said, 'Don't look back.
You can never look back.'"

- Don Henley, "The Boys of Summer"

"Do not go gentle into that good night,
Old age should burn and rave at close of day;
Rage, rage against the dying of the light.

Though wise men at their end know dark is right,
Because their words had forked no lightning they
Do not go gentle into that good night.

Good men, the last wave by, crying how bright
Their frail deeds might have danced in a green bay,
Rage, rage against the dying of the light.

Wild men who caught and sang the sun in flight,
And learn, too late, they grieved it on its way,
Do not go gentle into that good night.

Grave men, near death, who see with blinding sight
Blind eyes could blaze like meteors and be gay,
Rage, rage against the dying of the light.

And you, my father, there on the sad height,
Curse, bless me now with your fierce tears, I pray.
Do not go gentle into that good night.
Rage, rage against the dying of the light."

- Dylan Thomas, "Do Not Go Gentle into that Good Night"

"Don't stop thinking about tomorrow.
Don't stop, it'll soon be here.
It'll be better than before.
Yesterday's gone, yesterday's gone."

- Fleetwood Mac, "Don't Stop"

Chapter XXXI

Move-In Day

"Well I'm older now and still running against the wind."

- Bob Seger, "Against the Wind"

I was welcomed to Salem State College on September 1, 2008 by a crisp, cool ocean breeze that just couldn't seem to decide which direction to blow. It was one of those winds that the poet inside all of us just understands to be metaphorical. Metaphorical for what, I don't know. Perhaps it represented the final bit of resistance left in my path toward my ultimate goal. Perhaps it was a chance to allow the anxieties of my past to drift casually away. Maybe this wild wind stood for the changing direction of my life – as if the winds would finally be at my back. Perhaps there was no metaphor at all, but what fun would that be? Just ask Bob Seger.

As I jogged up and down the side streets surrounding my new college, I felt freer than I had felt in quite some time. My feet tied tightly into my New Balance running shoes felt lighter than air and for the first time in a while, I felt as though I was training for a purpose – maybe even a purpose greater than basketball. For me, that brief jog was the culmination of the hundreds of runs I had been on during my two-year hiatus from basketball, of the countless hours of work I had devoted to the weight room to become a bigger, faster, and stronger athlete, and most of all, of the hundreds of thousands of shots I had taken to perfect my art for some far-off second chance that might never come. As I ran through the streets of Salem, a single thought consumed me, blazing in my mind with a vehemence which I had never felt before: I had sought a change like I had done (or thought about doing) so many times previously in my life; however, this time, I followed through.

*****

The rest of the day following my run, I couldn't shake the smile from my face. I remember telling Sarah that I couldn't put into words how I felt, which is unusual for me. To this day I still cannot seem to find the right words. It was like I was overcome by excitement and zeal for my new situation, appreciation for Sarah and her urging me to come to Salem, a sense of accomplishment for actually making the change to Salem State, and even pride for my new school, all at once. I suppose even that jumble of emotion doesn't do that unique feeling any justice.

My first day as a Salem State Viking ended with an interesting encounter. As Sarah and I walked back from dinner at the dining hall, we bumped into two of her friends from her freshman year. They seemed overjoyed to meet me and they informed me how they were so excited for the upcoming basketball season because they had heard that I was a pretty good player. I suppose I felt a bit like a celebrity for that brief moment, perhaps the way my former teammates at Boston College felt all the time. Truthfully, I soaked in that conversation and that flattery, enjoying it for a short time, but as soon as we parted ways with them, I reminded myself why I was at Salem State – to achieve that *something* that had eluded my reach for far too long, that *something* that I would put into words only a few short months later.

Chapter XXXII

A Day that will Live in Infamy

"Father of mine, tell me where have you been.
You know I just closed my eyes and my whole world disappeared."

- Everclear, "Father of Mine"

I'm sure everyone has heard the classic expression "when it rains, it pours." I don't believe that that statement applies to anyone more directly than me. When the first day of basketball try-outs rolled around on October 15th, it was raining buckets.

For the first few months of the school year, I had maintained a relatively close contact with Coach Harvey, despite the fact that he wasn't actually my coach yet. I would try to stop by a few times a week and check in with him, tell him how pick-up games were going, talk about classes, or just "shoot the shit." Whenever we had team meetings or other compliance-based meetings, Coach would call me ahead of time to remind me, an indication that I was already a member of the team in his mind.

I remember sitting in his office one day discussing the probable roster for the upcoming season. The team was losing some pretty talented players, not to mention a number of seniors with seasoned leadership qualities, and we were conversing about who would fill these roles. Coach indicated that he had his mind set on most of the roster already and that the remaining five or six roster spots would be filled based on the try-outs. Surprised, I asked him if he thought there would even be five or six other guys to choose from at the try-out. He laughed, saying, "Just wait and see." I couldn't believe my eyes when I walked into Twohig Gymnasium on October 15th.

*****

I decided to go home for the weekend before my basketball try-outs to relax and prepare myself for a good week of practice; however, when I returned home, something seemed *off*. I remember the house feeling a bit *cold* that weekend – at least more unwelcoming than usual. My parents, especially, were acting strangely. My mother hadn't said more than a word to me when I walked through the door and I noticed that her eyes were red, as if she'd been crying. My father never moved from the coach nor averted his eyes from the television.

I was awoken on Saturday morning by my brother, Tyler, also home from college, who had come into my room holding a piece of paper. The note, from my father, said that he had something that he needed to tell us, and that he'd speak with us later in the evening. Immediately, I called my mother, who had gone to New York City Friday night with my sister, Kelsey, where Kelsey was shooting a movie trailer. With the grimmest of ideas swirling in my mind, I begged her to explain to me the nature of my father's vague note. As I asked her, I heard her begin to weep, painstakingly trying to mask her cries with fake coughs and exaggerated sighs. "We'll all talk tomorrow morning when we get back," was all she said before she hung up.

Naturally, my brother and I began speculating about the situation at hand. After brainstorming for a few minutes, we decided that there were only a few possible things that could cause our parents to act so out of the ordinary. We decided that either someone in our family had passed away, that my parents were filing for bankruptcy, that we had lost our family business, or that someone in our family was sick. My brother and I understood fully, however, that we were both ignoring the 10-ton African elephant looming menacingly in the corner of the room.

It was like looking into a mirror, and I imagine the same was true for Tyler, as we stood looking at each other in our kitchen, solemn-faced, two scared little boys stuck behind hardened, expressionless exteriors, each refusing to accept what we silently acknowledged to be truth.

The next morning, my sisters woke me up early, telling me that my parents needed to talk to all of us. When we walked into the family room, I immediately noticed my mother and father sitting on opposite ends of the room, my mother's head buried in her hands, her body heaving up and down as she shed silent tears.

"What's going on," I asked, attempting to cast my collectedness over the room to show my younger siblings that everything was going to be okay – that it just had to be okay.

"Sit down guys," my father said, "I have something I need to tell you all. Recently, I did something I'm not proud of. Well, I... I...," my hero stammered.

"What the hell did you do?" Kelsey screamed, sending shockwaves up and down my spine. Her six-word question transformed from the angry and violent outburst of a child to the painful inquiry of a young woman whose world was crashing down around her all in one breath. The yelp that at first sounded so barbaric almost melted into a puddle of anguish and defeat as the words forming her question trailed off, leaving a sullen fog sinking over the room.

"I haven't been faithful to my marriage," my former hero, now a mouse of a man, squeaked out, as he shrunk into nothingness in my mind. "I've been having an affair for over a year."

"He's been sleeping with another woman," was the outburst that came in-between sobs from my mother. Her eruption was like the first quake of thunder after a bolt of lightening strikes the ground in your backyard. Loud. Agonizing. Though it lasts for only seconds, you say a lifetime's worth of prayers that it will end immediately. My father's confession was the lightening that left me speechless and my mother's condemnation was the thunder that broke my heart.

Tears welled in my eyes, threatening to overflow the retaining wall that somehow held them in, as I refused to look at my father. I knew I needed to be strong for my siblings. I could feel their eyes on me. I heard my sisters begin to break down, Kelsey wailing, Codi weeping. I looked at my brother and oddly enough, in the moment, I found myself overcome by a feeling of how proud of him I was. I watched his face, dispassionate, as he tried with all of his strength to maintain his composure. He was doing it for me, I knew that much. He understood the burden I felt and tried to share the load with me. Tears began streaming down my face as I stared into his eyes; his lip began to quiver, simultaneously, tears following shortly thereafter. In this moment of utter chaos, when the threads that bound our family tightly together seemed to be coming undone, I found myself overcome with pride at the man my brother had become, at the way my sisters, early in their teen years, were able to accept this news, and most importantly, at the way, in that instant, my mother had become my hero. I knew that the five of us would have no problem weaving our threads even tighter than before. For the next few minutes, we all shared tears.

*****

When I returned to Salem State the next day, I was so distraught that the thought of trying out for a basketball team seemed almost inconsequential. I decided that I needed to tell Coach what had happened the day before to let him know where my head was.

When I explained the weekend's occurrences to him, he remained quiet for a moment and then said, "Brennan, unfortunately sometimes things happen in life that we have no control over and we can't blame ourselves for them. The most important thing you can do now is just be there for your mom and your sisters. They are the ones who need you the most. And the other thing is this: you obviously lost a lot of respect for your father – you might never respect him again – but you have to remember that he is still your father. He still loves you despite what he did."

I remember just nodding my head, once again fighting back tears.

"Let me remind you, though you might not be ready for it right now, basketball might be a way out for you. It might offer you that bit of solace that you need. I know, for me, when I step out onto the court, all of my outside problems disappear. When I'm between the lines, basketball's the only thing that matters."

I agreed with Coach and truthfully, I often feel the same way. I remembered something from a book I recently read, entitled *The Road to Blue Heaven: An Insider's Diary of North Carolina's 2007 Basketball Season*, written by a former North Carolina player, Wes Miller. Wes described how "on-court" problems often follow him off the court; however, he said that "off-court" problems are resolved by being on the court. I suppose I agree with that concept. Whenever something is bothering me, I can usually put it into perspective and come to a resolution by being on the basketball court, shooting, and thinking clearly.

A few days later, I walked into the James Twohig Gymnasium at Salem State for the first day of try-outs still very broken-up emotionally over what had happened the past weekend, a rain cloud hovering above my head in cartoon-like fashion. However, as I mentioned, it wasn't just raining that October 15th; it was pouring.

To my astonishment, there were nearly 30 guys in the gym, each trying to make the team. A few days earlier, Coach had told me that he would try to weed out the guys who didn't belong by doing a few simple running drills and scrimmages. As we began the running, I found that I was extremely sluggish, probably a result of getting no sleep the few nights leading up to the try-out for obvious reasons. The more we ran, the more my legs felt like Jell-O and as we made teams for scrimmages, my head began to throb, feeling like it was expanding at an "exponential rate." Suddenly, as we began the scrimmage, I realized that I couldn't see anything; my vision had literally failed.

This phenomenon, which has only happened to me a few times in my life, probably fewer than 10 times, is called an "aura," a perceptual disturbance experienced by some migraine headache sufferers before a migraine attack. Unfortunately for me, I am one of the 6-15 % of adult males who suffers from migraine headaches, and one of the even smaller percentage of these people who experiences "auras" before an attack. My aura has always been the loss of vision. When a migraine is about to set in, I will lose the ability to see more than a few inches in front of my face and also experience terrible double vision or tunnel vision. Migraines are probably the most painful thing I have ever experienced, as anyone who has ever had one can attest to. During migraine attacks, I actually look forward to vomiting because it relieves the pressure on my brain momentarily and eases the pain for a few minutes. Most typically, I get migraines when I am overly stressed, and as one might expect, I was a bit stressed-out during the week of October 15th.

Needless to say, the first day of try-outs was a complete and total disaster for me. After the two-hour practice, I stumbled out of the gym into the cold fall night, fell to the ground, and vomited, temporarily relieving the pain I was in, allowing myself time to get back to my dorm before the pain set in again.

The next morning, while it was ironically raining, I stopped in to see Coach Harvey to explain to him that I was obviously under a lot of stress then and that I had a migraine during the try-out. I was hoping that he would understand that I was not on my game, so to speak, because of all of the outside factors working against me. Thankfully, he reassured me of his confidence in me, explained that regardless of how well or poorly I played during the try-out that I was already on the team, and that he was almost positive that I could start every game for the team during the season. Nevertheless, my first few days with Salem Sate basketball were soggy.

Chapter XXXIII

Throwing Away my Mask

"To be nobody but yourself in a world which is doing its best,
night and day, to make you everybody else – means to fight the hardest
battle which any human being can fight; and never stop fighting."

- e.e. cummings, *A Poet's Advice*

Despite the fact that I had performed so lousily in my first few days of practice, Coach had told me that I was on the basketball team at Salem State. I was on the basketball team at Salem State where I could be the impact player I knew that I could be. I remember feeling an unbelievable sense of accomplishment and moreover, relief at the fact that I had finally accomplished this goal. It felt as though a weight was lifted off of my shoulders and despite the fact that things were spinning so rapidly out of control in my life off the court, everything seemed to just slow down and make sense for a minute. I felt a moment's clarity in a world that's meaning had suddenly become hazy and for the first time in a while, I was able to simply let my guard down.

I remember sitting in an American Literature class during the second semester of my first year at Salem State and reading a poem entitled "We Wear the Mask," by Paul Laurence Dunbar, which I felt truly summed up my experience with the Boston College Basketball program, and furthermore, expressed how I felt after making the team at Salem. The following is an excerpt from the 1896 poem:

> We wear the mask that grins and lies,
> It hides our cheeks and shades our eyes,—
> This debt we pay to human guile;
> With torn and bleeding hearts we smile,
> And mouth with myriad subtleties.

Why should the world be over-wise,
In counting all our tears and sighs?
Nay, let them only see us, while
We wear the mask.

Probably the most unique and important aspect of this poem is that the poem is virtually subjectless – or perhaps appropriate for any/every subject. As readers, we have the authority to assign any subject to the "we" that Dunbar refers to – perhaps any "we" that we as readers have felt like we belong with. A woman might read this and say that she truly relates to the poem – that she walks through life "wearing a mask" to be someone or something that she isn't or simply to hide a life full of pain or sorrow. Gays might feel the same way. Perhaps Jews. Maybe Muslims. Interestingly enough, I feel like I have "worn the mask" at times in my own life, most notably, during my time with BC Basketball.

Throughout the season at BC, I felt like I was forced to smile – to wear the mask – just to fit in and cover up the fact that I really was never happy on the team. One of the most satisfying accomplishments of my life was making the basketball team at Salem and securing the feeling that I could finally remove my mask and just be happy with where I was.

Chapter XXXIV

My First Taste of Viking Basketball

"The way to gain a good reputation is to
endeavor to be what you desire to appear."

- Socrates

Despite getting off to a rough start with Salem State Basketball, I soon found myself fitting in quite nicely with the team. I found myself becoming friends with every member of my team, something reminiscent of high school sports. More importantly for me, however, was that it appeared that each of my teammates liked me as well and enjoyed having me as a member of the program.

On the third day of practice, Coach began to put in our "offense." I say "offense" simply because our offense was by no means a traditional set offense. Our offense was strictly a motion-based, move-without-the-ball, cut, screen, and be basketball-savvy offense. Coach discouraged too much dribbling, quick shots, and most of all (and most importantly to me), quick drives to the hoop from the top or the wings. Moreover, he always preached that we should give up a good shot for a great one. It was literally as simple as that. No plays. No sets. No structure. And thus, no stiffness or rigidity in the offensive flow. Just a flowing, motion offense.

This was quite a shock for me because I have always played on teams that have had multiple sets and a multitude of different plays in each set. In fact, at Boston College, we had so many plays that I was actually unable to learn them all by the end of the season!

Surprisingly, however, this "motion offense," as Coach aptly named it, took quite a bit of time to "master," though I'd truthfully say we never completely mastered it. It was the kind of offense that takes months and months of practice to fully pick up, mostly because to master a motion-based offense, you have to be able to anticipate what your teammates are going to do. To be able to anticipate their actions, you have to be able to anticipate their thoughts. To be able to anticipate the thoughts of your teammates takes a significant amount of practice, and more importantly, a significant amount of togetherness – we spent two or three hours together almost every day for six and a half months running this offense and we still weren't able to master it. Truthfully, I don't think a team can ever really perfect this offense.

I also think, however, that this inability for our own team to master our offense is partially what makes the offense so effective. Just think about it. How can an opposing coach scout our offense when it looks completely different each and every time down the court? If we barely know what our teammates are going to do, how could our opponents have any idea of what was about to hit them? I suppose it's the same reason a normal-stance fighter will sometimes switch to become a southpaw during the middle of a fight – to surprise the opponent and give him a look he has not prepared for. Our offense was very similar to this fighter. Sometimes we'd fight normal-stance. Other times, we'd go southpaw. Sometimes we'd stand backwards. And other times, we'd stand on our hands. In other words, our offense was going to look different every game and moreover, every possession, so our opponents never knew what look we were going to give them.

When Coach Harvey began implementing the beginnings of the "motion offense" on day three of the young season, we still had approximately 25 guys in the gym, even despite the first round of "cuts" where Coach trimmed the number from the mid 30s to only 25. When the time arrived for Coach to begin teaching us the offense, he called out five players to demonstrate the offense for the rest of the team – Dylan Holmes, our center captain and defending conference player of the year, Stevie Celestin, one of our tri-captains, Ricky Ogboin, the third of our captains, Nick Linear, a returning sophomore forward from whom we expected greatness, and me, who felt like all eyes were on me and all whispers about me.

There was a perceived negative electricity in the gym as I walked away from the main group out onto the floor to take the reins of the offense at the point guard position. I imagined that questions and comments about why I was out there were being flung around the gymnasium like spitballs in a middle school cafeteria. *He hasn't even done anything yet. So what if he played at BC. Let him prove himself first.* Truth be told, most guys were probably more worried about learning the offense and less concerned with why Coach had chosen me to run the point; however, in my mind, all eyes were on me.

I tried to absorb everything Coach preached on that first day of offense, but my mind was more focused on the conversation I would have with Coach at the end of practice.

After our usual end-of-practice huddle broke, I made my way through the droves of people playing one-on-one, each one desperately trying to prove his worth and snatch up one of the last few roster spots for the season, until I found Coach Harvey standing in the doorway of Twohig Gymnasium. I approached him, trying my best to emanate confidence, and told him flat-out that I didn't want to be given anything, but rather, that I wanted to earn everything I got in his program. I told him that if I earn a starting role on the team then I will most certainly accept the responsibility; however, if I am not one of the best five players on the team, I will do what is best for the team and come off the bench. Either way, I told him, I certainly didn't want to "rest on my laurels" and be handed a starting job because I was in the right place at the right time at BC and made *that* team. In my mind, *that* team had absolutely nothing to do with *this* team. Furthermore, I told him that my number one priority on this team was to gain the respect of my teammates, not to inherit their resentment at the fact that I was given a role on the team due to my past accomplishments.

Coach seemed a bit surprised to hear these words coming out of my mouth. I think he just assumed that I would be starting on his team and that everyone else understood this as well. Nevertheless, he obliged to honor my concern and agreed to let Brian Marvie, a returning junior point guard and the player who was expected to run the point for the 2008-2009 campaign, manage the offense during drills and offensive installments.

As we parted ways after our conversation on day three, I assured Coach that I would never again give up a starting role – the job was mine and I was going to earn it.

Chapter XXXV

Division III Vs. Division I

"It is not how big you are, it is how big you play."

- Unknown Author

As the games of the 2008-2009 season began, I found myself in the starting lineup, as I had hoped I would. However, surprisingly, I was starting at the shooting guard, or 2-guard, position, rather than the point guard, or 1-guard, spot.

After about two weeks of practice, Coach Harvey called me into his office where he, Coach Jones, and Coach Manderson were sitting and discussing the progress of the team. When I entered his office and sat down, Coach Harv asked me how I felt I was playing. Naturally – and probably instinctively – I told him that I thought I was playing well, but that there was certainly room for improvement. He seemed surprised when I told him that I still didn't feel *right* running the point.

"I've noticed," he said chuckling. "Do you think you're struggling a bit just because of the level of competition?"

I laughed nervously and shifted in my seat, saying, "Well, I'm probably just having a difficult time adjusting to the position."

"What do you mean 'adjusting'?" Coach replied.

"Well I've never played point guard before, outside of summer league anyway," I said.

"Really?" he mumbled, his chin resting in the open palm of his hand, his fingers wrapping around his jaw line, and his index finger running up the side of his face.

"Really," I managed, a bit confused at his reaction. He must have assumed because of my size and quickness that I was a point guard my whole career. After all, he never really scouted me the way a coach would scout an incoming freshman recruit, but rather, he probably more-or-less took the "Well-If-He-Can-Play-At-BC Approach" and assumed if I could make that team, I could make his team. Furthermore, he must have assumed that there was no way I could have made that team as a shooting guard standing only 6' tall (most Division I shooting guards will be between 6' 3" and 6' 5"). What's a bit ironic, however, is that the coaching staff at Boston College made a very similar assumption. For the first few days of practice at BC, I ran the third-string point guard position and it wasn't until I met with Coach Murphy and requested a run at the shooting guard spot that the change happened.

"I think I might be able to help the team a bit more from the shooting guard spot. I know Stevie is a great 2-guard but he has a much better handle on the ball than I do and he might be even more effective at the point guard," I said.

"Agreed," Coach responded, smiling wryly at the realization of the error of his assumption. "I don't know if you'll start at the 2-guard because we have a lot of talent there, but you'll certainly still get significant minutes."

I acknowledged Coach's words and left the gym knowing wholeheartedly that I would start for this team. When the first game finally arrived on November 18th, I was the team's starting shooting guard.

*****

Even as the games began early in our season, I had already noticed quite a few significant differences between Salem State Basketball and Boston College Basketball. First and foremost, I noticed an extreme difference between the two schools' basketball locker rooms. As I have already described, the locker room at BC was, in a word, breathtaking. It had leather couches, carpeted and hardwood floors, a big screen television, and individual lockers with our names and pictures on them. Salem State College's basketball locker room was, needless to say, not as glorious. In fact, until the night of our first game (the season began on October 15th and the games began November 18th), I had never even seen the inside of our locker room. At Salem, we would simply bring our bags and clothes into the gym and change in the bleachers. When I finally did grace the inside of the locker room, I had to laugh because the locker room was exactly like the kind we had in high school – small, concrete floors, old metal lockers, and certainly no Playstation 3. Moreover, we shared a locker room with the Women's Field Hockey team!

Furthermore, on the night of our first game, as I walked into the locker room for the first time, I was surprised not to find my uniform hanging in my locker. At this point, I noticed the second major difference between Divisions I and III – people don't do everything for you! I had to walk down to the trainer's room to get my own uniform. Moreover, the uniforms weren't the new, custom-ordered, name embroidered on the back type of uniforms that we received at Boston College, but rather, they were just the same uniforms that the team had worn the year before and what size uniform you got depended on what number you were assigned. I wore number 10 (the same number I wore at BC) and both my jersey and shorts were extremely large and loose-fitting. In fact, I had to cut the drawstring just to make the shorts fit me. We also got a shooting shirt, similar to Boston College; however, the shooting shirts we got at Salem weren't quite as *expensive* as the BC variety. At BC we were given heavy, zip-up shooting shirts that displayed a sewn-on patch of an eagle on the front, but at Salem, we simply wore an orange, Under Armour, long-sleeve t-shirt for warm-ups. Finally, contrary to the six or seven pairs of new shoes we got at Boston College, we only received one pair at Salem, which had to last the entire season! (It's difficult to whine about only getting one pair of free shoes because it certainly beats the hell out of paying $150 for my own shoes! Just bear with the whining.)

Yet another difference between Division III ball at Salem State and Division I ball at Boston College was the difference in venue. While at Boston College, I was fortunate enough to have the opportunity to play (well, watch from a close seat) at some of the most famous arenas in the country – Cameron Indoor at Duke, the Dean Dome at UNC and even our own gym, Conte Forum. On the contrary, at Salem State, the nicest gym I played at all year might have been Framingham State College (and this is most definitely no knock on FSC; they really do have a nice gym; however, there have never been any ESPN cameras inside!). Moreover, the way we traveled was a bit different, too. Obviously, at BC we flew almost everywhere we played, excluding the TD Garden, of course. However, at Salem, we didn't fly to a single game. In fact, we made the 4+ hour bus ride to play at MCLA and twice made even longer rides later in the season.

Probably the most notable difference in the away games between the two schools, however, was the difference in the amount of meal money we received. At Boston College, as I've mentioned, we would sometimes receive upwards of $60 for food for a two-day trip. At Salem State, we typically got $7 for food for road games (for the really far ones we might get $11!). There was almost a full-scale riot the first time I mentioned how much money we would be given at BC for meal money to my Salem teammates. Coach could only laugh and yell, "State school, gentlemen." Furthermore, at Salem, away games were never two or three day affairs as they were at Boston College. At Salem, if we had a game scheduled for 7:00 p.m., we would leave Salem at 4:30 the same day, play the game, and return to Salem that same night. Needless to say, traveling four hours to MCLA for a 7:00 p.m. game and then returning the same four hours the very same night never made for a very appetizing trip.

The next major differences between the two programs in which I spent a significant amount of time over the last few years were the weight rooms and training staffs. At Boston College, the weight room was simply state-of-the-art. In fact, as I've previously mentioned, athletes had their very own weight-training facility. At Salem, on the other hand, we shared a very small, often over-crowded weight room with all of the students and faculty in the school. Furthermore, the weight room at BC came complete with three personal trainers and free recovery bars and protein shakes. At Salem, it didn't. Luckily for me, however, I was able to translate a lot of the workouts and exercises that I learned while at BC to my time at Salem in the Salem State weight room.

Sticking with the theme of finding differences in the athletics facilities at my two respective schools, I found another major difference in the actual gyms themselves at BC and Salem State. At Boston College, we played in Silvio O. Conte Forum, a beautiful arena that could pack about 9,000 people around the court and frequently played host to ESPN personalities, like Erin Andrews. At Salem, on the other hand, we played in Twohig Gymnasium, which was extremely nice as far as gymnasiums go, but in the end, it was simply a gym, not much unlike the gym I played at in high school. Probably the biggest difference between the two gyms was the actual basketball courts. At BC, the Conte Forum floor was used solely for Men's and Women's Basketball games. Very rarely did we even practice on the Conte Forum floor, excluding pre-game walk-throughs. At Salem, however, Twohig Gymnasium basketball court was used for just about everything under the sun. The school used the basketball court for Men's and Women's Basketball, Volleyball, Lacrosse practice, Baseball and Softball practices, physical education classes, guest speakers, community involvement activities, and a whole host of other activities, so needless to say, the court became quite worn out by the end of the season. During practices, especially nearing the end of the season, the gym floor began to resemble an ice hockey rink more than a basketball court in terms of its traction. Frequently throughout the course of a game I would have to wipe the bottoms of my shoes to get the layers of dirt and dust off. My mother always jokes that she never has any problem locating me on the basketball court because I'm the one who's always bending down to wipe my shoes (and then putting my fingers in my mouth to get my fingers sticky).

Let's recap. At Boston College, I had an astonishing locker room, pristine uniforms with my name embroidered on the back, and people to make sure my uniform was hanging in my locker before every game and that my practice gear was in my locker before every practice. At Boston College, I played at some of the most spectacular arenas in the country, flew to every destination at which we played, and received more meal money than I would ever possibly need. At Boston College, I, as an athlete, got my own private weight room, had personal trainers to assist me on every step of the way, was privy to free recovery bars and protein shakes, and had the chance to play basketball in front of 9,000 screaming people on Silvio O. Conte Forum court. At Salem State, my rarely-seen locker room was run down, had concrete floors, and the majority of the lockers wouldn't close. At Salem State, my uniform was a year-to-year hand-me-down and my name wasn't displayed across the back of my shoulders. At Salem State, I shared a weight room with every other student and faculty member of the college. At Salem State, I never flew in an airplane and I only received $7 for meal money each away game. At Salem State, I played on Twohig Gymnasium's slippery, dusty floor which every other student was allowed to use, and I played in front of only hundreds of people each game.

People might call me crazy but I'd choose Salem State College over Boston College any and every day of the week because Salem State Basketball did one thing that Boston College Basketball could never do – it made me happy.

*****

Probably one of my favorite moments throughout the entire season came very early in the season as we were traveling to Wheaton College for our fourth game of the year. We left Salem at 4:00 p.m. and began the one hour and 20 minute trip to Norton, MA for our 7:00 p.m. tip-off against Wheaton. Unfortunately, we didn't take into account the fact that we would be heading directly into the teeth of rush hour traffic. About 30 minutes into our trip we came to a grinding halt and we soon realized that there would be no way that we would make it to Wheaton by game time. Coach Harvey got on the phone and called Wheaton's athletic director and explained to him that we would be there as soon as we could but that we couldn't promise that we'd be there by game time. As the minutes passed and we inched ever closer to Wheaton along I-93, Coach told us that we had to change on the bus and those of us who needed our ankles taped needed to do it on the bus, as well. The subsequent minutes will be a memory that I will always have because of the complete and utter lunacy of it all. There were 14 guys on our team, each one trying frantically to get dressed on a moving bus in the dark, while the guy next to him was trying to do the same in the exact same space. People were bumping into each other, falling over, losing shoes under the bus seats, and fighting over who was next in line to get taped up. I remember just laughing to myself, thinking what this situation would look like to a car stuck in traffic next to us on the highway. When I finished getting dressed, I looked up to the front of the bus to where Coach Harvey was sitting, turned around, facing us. He laughed and yelled, "Put this in your book!"

I remember thinking at that moment that *this* – this team environment, this togetherness, and this friendship – was what I had signed up for. *This* was exactly the reason I had transferred to Salem State College to play Division III basketball. I knew that something like this would have never happened at BC. We would never have had to change on the bus at BC. We would never have arrived at the opponent's gym at 6:50 for a 7:00 game while at BC, and we certainly would never have begun a game at BC with only five minutes of warm-ups. All of those things are what made Salem State so perfect for me. We ended up beginning that night's game as sluggish as ever and fell behind quickly, trailing by double digits right out of the gates. We made a nice push late in the second half to cut the deficit to only one point, but Wheaton's 55% three-point field goal percentage was too much for us to overcome in the end and we lost by 16. But the beauty of that night is that years from now, I probably won't remember many of the details from the game itself; however, I can say without even the slightest shadow of doubt that I will never forget the events leading up to game time on November 25th, 2008.

Chapter XXXVI

Bitten by the Injury Bug

"The difference between a successful person and others is not
a lack of strength, not a lack of knowledge, but rather a lack of will."

- Vince Lombardi

Up until January 26th, 2009, my season at Salem State was going just the way I had envisioned it would go. We were out in front of our conference, leading the MASCAC with a 14-3 record, and playing some pretty good basketball, despite dropping our last game to league rival, Bridgewater State. I was still starting at the 2-guard and playing about 22 minutes per game, averaging just around eight points per contest, and I had been named to the Salem State Christmas Classic All-Tournament Team. I felt in my heart of hearts, though, that I could be performing more effectively; however, I was still so thrilled to be starting, playing well, and contributing to a team that was winning basketball games that I put all of my personal concerns on the backburner and just concentrated on helping to win basketball games for my team – which, as I said, we had been doing extremely effectively up to this point.

Practice on January 26th, 2009, my 21st birthday, began just as normally as ever. We ran our usual "Celtic Drill" to get our legs loose and then transitioned into a one-on-one drill we frequently did during practices to improve our one-on-one skills – both offensively and defensively. When it was my turn to play defense, I stepped up to defend Brian Marvie, one of our point guards, and attempted to force him to his left hand. He made a nice, quick move to get back to his right and powered up for a right-handed lay-up. Knowing that I had been beaten off the dribble, I should have attempted to swipe for the ball to prevent Brian from scoring; however, forgetting that I am only 6' tall and don't jump well, I tried to leap up and block his shot. I jumped for the block, missed, and watched his lay-up fall through the rim; however, as I came back down from my leap, my left foot landed awkwardly on Brian's foot and I collapsed, rolling all of my body weight over my ankle to the sickening pop of snapping tendons. The pain was instant and viciously intense, shooting up my leg and crippling my body. I sat up and slammed my fists against the ground in agony and then, using my arms, I dragged myself off the court and grabbed my ankle along the baseline. The trainers were over to me within seconds, bags of ice already in hand. They helped me up and I hobbled over to the sideline using them as crutches. When I got to the sideline, they took off my shoe (which is usually not smart with an ankle roll; however, mine was so severe that the swelling would have been terrible either way) and instantly my ankle swelled to four or five times its normal size. I have sprained my ankles before, once playing basketball in middle school and once as a senior wide-receiver in football season, but never before had the swelling been this dramatic. In fact, the swelling was so severe that I couldn't have an x-ray for almost a full week because there would have been no way the doctors could have seen the ankle bone through all the swelling (according to our trainers).

A week later I went to the hospital to have my ankle x-rayed and to determine the length of time I would have to miss. I was still in tremendous pain and couldn't put even the slightest bit of pressure on my foot. In fact, I couldn't even move my foot without severe pain. After seeing the doctor, I was thrilled to learn that my ankle wasn't broken; however, he told me that with an ankle sprain this bad, it might have actually been better if I had broken it because that way, the recovery time might have been shorter. He told me that it would take me 4-6 weeks before I could even think about playing again and that it might even take those same 4-6 weeks before I could begin any rehab. I was determined to be back on my feet and playing by the next Bridgewater game, which was only four weeks away on February 17th.

*****

For the next two or three weeks, I was extremely careful not to put too much pressure on my foot or step the wrong way (this was all made far more difficult by the fact that it was winter on the North Shore, which means there was a surplus of ice and snow to make crutching around a nightmare). Each day during practice, while my team was practicing in the gym, I would totter downstairs to the basement of the O'Keefe Athletic Center to the training room where I would aggressively (as aggressively as possible, anyway) treat my ankle injury.

My treatments began with just a heaping helping of ice, on and off for 30 minutes at a time. After a few days of icing, I began to use stimulation treatment (the same thing I used to treat my aching shoulder at Boston College). One of the trainers – Brian, James, Naoko, or Natsuko – would wrap my ankle in ice and apply the stim-pads to allow an electrical current to flush out some of the swelling in my ankle. After about a week of just doing stim-treatment, I began to do ice bath treatments and laser treatments, which are just more intense treatment methods to reduce swelling.

One of the most painful treatments I received was a treatment called "milking" my ankle. One of the trainers would put lotion on my ankle, raise it up above his or her head, and begin firmly squeezing the fluid out of my ankle. They would run their thumbs down my foot, from toes to ankle, forcing the swelling out of my foot. With all of the swelling being forced out of my foot and ankle and toward my lower leg, I was shocked to see my calves and shins begin to turn yellow and purple. Each of these treatments – ice, electric stimulation, laser, and milking – was an attempt to reduce the swelling in my ankle enough so that I could begin to put significant pressure on it, move and bend it a little more, and ultimately, begin biking and lightly jogging on it again. After two and a half weeks of aggressive treatment, I was able to ride the exercise bike for a few minutes and walk semi-normally without crutches. The trainers were astonished at how quickly I was recovering from such a severe ankle injury, though they were all quick to say that their training and treatment skills were the reason for my quick recovery!

Three days before the Bridgewater State game, while at our game against Fitchburg State out in Fitchburg, MA, I decided to attempt to walk normally, without my crutches. Surprisingly, I was able to walk relatively normally, and decided that the next day at practice I would attempt to jog and run a little with the trainers. The next day, Brian had me jumping to do wall-taps, doing lunges across the gym, and running from the baseline to the elbow for a jump shot, shuffling from elbow to elbow, and then sprinting back to the baseline. I was astonished at how quickly my ankle went from unable to support my body weight to able to support light running. After that day of treatment, I was extremely sore, but I called Coach anyway and told him that I was going to be ready to play in the Bridgewater game (which, as it turned out, was one of the biggest games of the year because if we lost again to Bridgewater, we wouldn't have had a chance to win the regular season championship for our conference).

*****

On February 17th, I had my ankles taped up tightly, laced up my Nike Hyperdunk shoes, took five Ibuprofens, and prepared myself mentally for the biggest game of our season against our archrivals, the Bridgewater State Bears. Coach had told me before the game that I would not be starting, for obvious reasons, but that I would come off the bench a little later in the game.

As the game started, we got out to a commanding lead and played an extremely strong first 10 minutes of basketball. At about the 10-minute mark, Coach subbed me into the game. My heart was pounding because I didn't know how well my ankle was going to hold up and I knew that if I stepped or landed awkwardly, I might collapse the same way I did before. When I entered the game, I very quickly felt my legs turn heavy. I had forgotten, with all of my concern on my ankle, that my wind wouldn't be the same as it was four weeks ago, before I got hurt. Despite the fact that I was winded very quickly, I attempted to give my team the best four of five minutes that I could and then tell Coach that I needed to come out and catch my breath. The four minutes went relatively smoothly for me; I didn't touch the ball offensively, and because of Bridgewater's ability to match up well against us, we had been playing a zone which allowed me to remain relatively stationary and not put too much strain on my weak ankle. At about the four-minute mark, during perhaps the last trip down the court before Coach was going to take me out, I caught the ball on a swing and without hesitation, fired up a three-pointer that dropped in as if I hadn't missed a step. After I made the basket Coach took me out but for a short time, I felt like I was on cloud nine. I forgot about my throbbing ankle and was so wrapped up in the flow of the game that I didn't give my ankle a second thought until after the game.

Right before the half, Coach subbed me back in the game with us up eight points. As time was winding down in the half, I launched another deep three-pointer and made my second shot of the night to give us an 11-point halftime lead. Bridgewater made a nice push late in the second half to make it a three-point game, but our resiliency shined and we ended up holding on for an eight-point victory and we moved into a tie for first place atop our conference. I finished the game with seven points, adding a free throw to my two three-balls late in the contest.

After the game, my ankle was as sore as it had been since I began my treatment. It was throbbing so badly later that night that I actually had a hard time falling asleep. I was willing to deal with a little pain and swelling, though, because my comeback was in full swing and we were back on top of our conference once again. After the Bridgewater game we had one more regular season contest against Worcester State and then we would begin our conference tournament with a first round bye; however, none of us was prepared for what would shake the foundations of our team in the subsequent week. No ankle sprain in the history of sports could compare to the devastation we would face as a team on the night of February 26th, 2009.

Chapter XXXVII

The Massachusetts State College
Athletic Conference Tournament

"Defeat never comes to any man until he admits it."

- Josephus Daniels

February 26th, 2009 began as normally as any other day. I woke up and conducted my daily routine as I always had on a game day. I went to class, came back, caught a quick nap, and prepared myself mentally for my upcoming game. That night, at 7:00 p.m., we were to play Framingham State College, a team coming off an impressive 90-77 first-round victory over Worcester State, in the second round of the Massachusetts State College Athletic Conference tournament.

We dominated the Framingham State Rams in every aspect of basketball right from the opening tap. In fact, after I made my first free throw of the game to give us a 1-0 advantage, we never relinquished the lead for the entirety of the contest. We controlled the pace of the game throughout and dominated in every basketball category, holding the edge in points in the paint, points off of turnovers, bench points, fast-break points, rebounds, and field goal percentage. At halftime, we had a commanding 45-24 lead and we never looked back. We ended up winning the game by a margin of 23 points, paced by an impressive game from one of our rising stars, Nick Linear, who scored 26 points. I finished the game with seven points – four free throws and a three-ball – but I was far more pleased with the team victory than anything else. After the game, everyone was ecstatic. We were jumping around and giving each other high fives of congratulations in the classroom where our team gathers after games and the coaching staff was extremely pleased by our efforts on the court. It seemed that we were coming together and playing our best basketball at the perfect time of the year.

Before we left the classroom to go be with our friends and families, Coach Harvey offered us one caveat. He urged us to remember that we had a conference championship game against Bridgewater State in only two days and with a win in that game we would receive an automatic bid to the NCAA Division III national tournament. Thus, he told us to remember to be responsible and, in words not so eloquent, not to do anything stupid that night. Unfortunately, some of my teammates didn't heed this warning.

*****

I was awoken Friday morning, February 27th, at 10:30 by the violent vibrate of my cell phone, indicating that I had received a text message. I wasn't in class that morning because when we picked classes at the end of the first semester, I, being an athlete, had the privilege of selecting my classes before any of the other students in the school. Thus, I was able to finagle my schedule so I only had classes on Tuesdays and Thursdays and therefore had Mondays, Wednesdays, and Fridays to relax, sleep in, catch up on homework, or just hang out.

When I rolled out of bed and grabbed my cell phone, I saw that the text was from Dylan and I was expecting the normal Dylan text – something along the lines of "Let's stay focused, have a great day of practice today, and win tomorrow night." Needless to say, I was dismayed and confused when I opened my phone and read, "We have to come together and pray now for our brother Jon. Team meeting at 11:30." I closed the phone and stood, silent, for a while, wondering what that text meant. Obviously something had happened to my teammate, Jon, but what?

When I arrived at the O'Keefe Center for our team meeting, all of my teammates were wearing the same sullen, dejected look on their faces. I saw Dylan and asked him what had happened. He told me that there had been a bad car accident late the night before and that a few of our teammates had been involved. I learned that Nick had been driving the car, had been banged up pretty badly in the accident, and had spent the night in the hospital because of his injuries. Bernard, one of our freshmen, was injured in the accident, too, hurting his knee, wrist, and thumb so severely that he was forced to miss the remainder of the season. The last of our teammates involved was Jon. Jon had taken the worst of the accident and was left in the hospital fighting for his life on a breathing machine. On the morning of February 27th, we weren't sure if Jon was going to survive.

We met with the Salem State Athletic Director a few minutes after everyone arrived to discuss the different scenarios and possibilities for the following night's game. The AD told us that we had a few options: A) not play the championship game against Bridgewater or B) play the game with heavy hearts (because Jon was in critical condition and neither Nick nor Bernard would be able to play due to their injuries). If we decided to choose option A, and not play the game, the MASCAC conference would be forced to choose a team to represent it in the national tournament, and because we and Bridgewater both finished with identical records atop the conference standings during the regular season, but we were the reason that no championship game was played, the conference would have no choice but to award the automatic bid to Bridgewater. On the other hand, if we played without conviction and our heads were elsewhere, as they would naturally be inclined to be, we would risk picking up another loss and finding ourselves "on the fence" to receive one of the few "at-large" bids to the national tournament (an at-large bid is an invitation to the tournament based on a team's outstanding overall record, despite the fact that that team was unsuccessful in winning its conference tournament and securing an automatic bid).

After some deliberation, we unanimously agreed that we had to play the game – if nothing else, *for* Jon. We decided that Jon was one of us – our brother. He had been with us from the beginning and we wanted him there, in spirit, at the end. He had been a part of our team through the grueling early-season practices when the season seemed so far away, when we were winning and assembling win streaks throughout the year, and when we were losing games, as well. He was as much a member of our team as anyone and he would want us to play that championship game for him. We knew that he would say that there was no way we had come all that way to forfeit the championship game and thus, we decided to play against Bridgewater the next night.

*****

As game time approached on Saturday, February 28th, none of us was truly ready to play a basketball game – especially a game of this magnitude. Everything we had worked so tirelessly for throughout the season was riding on the outcome of this MASCAC championship game, and needless to say, our heads were not in Twohig Gymnasium at all.

The game was an utter disaster right from the opening tip. Quite the contrary from the Framingham game only two nights before, we were dominated in almost every basketball category, including being on the wrong ends of the rebound margin, field goal percentage, three-point field goal percentage, and free throw percentage. At halftime we were trailing by eight points, however, it was an eight-point lead that felt like 28. Our play in the second half was equally as feeble and we ultimately lost the game by 11 points, 77-66.

After the game, we had to watch Bridgewater accept their MASCAC championship medals, and more importantly, their invitation to the NCAA national tournament, on our home court. Each one of us stood next to our bench as the procession was carried out in front of us, wrestling with a number of emotions – for me, both bitter melancholy and extreme frustration. The first emotion that sank in for me was the feeling of gloom. I was so upset and disheartened that all of the "blood, sweat, and tears," proverbially speaking, were for naught. In other words, everything we had worked for all season long – from the earliest days of try-outs until the final minutes of the MASCAC championship game – flew out the window with the loss to Bridgewater. We would not be the recipients of an automatic bid to the national tournament, and with six losses, our chances of receiving an at-large bid looked grim, too.

The next feeling that hit me like an oncoming locomotive was the aforementioned frustration. I felt almost ashamed to be feeling what I was feeling but nonetheless, I felt angry and resentful about the impact the accident had on our team. I felt like our teammates had let us down. They had made a very poor decision that night and because of their ill-advised choice, we didn't have one of our best players and thus, lost the biggest game of our season. From the moment I got to Salem, I wanted a chance to win the national championship. Up until that loss to Bridgewater, that goal was a very real, very viable possibility. Now, after that loss, their was a chance that we might not make the tournament at all, and despite the fact that we still had a chance to win the game after the accident, the events of the night of February 26th certainly hindered the play of our team and for that, I felt extremely angry.

Looking back on that night, I realize that my feelings were selfish because one of my teammates, and moreover, one of my friends, was fighting for his life in the hospital and I now certainly realize that a friend's life is far more important that any basketball dream; however, the choice my teammates made that night was a selfish one, too, and at the time, I was upset.

Ultimately, however, my selfish anger, my teammates' poor decision, and our loss to our archrivals all went by the wayside because on March 2nd, 2009, I learned that we had, in fact, received an at-large bid to the national tournament and that we'd be playing the Rochester Institute of Technology in the first round at Widener University in Chester, Pennsylvania. The better news, however, was that we were told that Jon was going to be okay and make a full recovery over the next few weeks.

Chapter XXXVIII

The Division III NCAA National Tournament

"No bird soars too high if he soars with his own wings."

- William Blake, "Proverbs of Hell," *The Marriage of Heaven and Hell*

The atmosphere in Widener University's Schwartz Athletic Center was absolutely electric as we prepared for our first-round game against the Rochester Institute of Technology. The music blasting from the loudspeakers coursed through my body, pumping adrenaline into my arms and legs, giving me that "elastic-muscles" feeling, as if I could have jumped out of the gym. The nerves running through my body made my stomach uneasy, but it was the kind of uneasiness that you wait your entire life to experience – the kind of restlessness that you can't put into words, but rather, because of the rarity and short-lived nature of the sensation, it eludes the lips of even the finest orators or the words of the most practiced wordsmiths. It is the kind of anxious unease that old men speak about when they say, "I don't even know how to describe the feeling," as they relive the pride of being enlisted to fight for the freedom of their country. It is the kind of anxious unease that your father speaks about when he says, "I didn't know how to feel" as he relives the first few moments of your life. It is the kind of restlessness that no matter how fiercely you shake your arms and legs or roll your neck or stretch your hamstrings, you cannot for the life of you shake the feeling – if anything, it grows even more intense.

The best way I can capture that particular sensation is by likening it to the kind of anxious anticipation of achieving the one thing that has occupied your every waking moment – every free thought your mind has had – for the entirety of your existence in this world. Imagine the one thing that has always eluded your outstretched arms – the one thing that you have sought tirelessly, maybe even grazed briefly with your reaching finger tips, but never quite been able to grasp tightly and press firmly against your body. Now imagine that same thing sitting directly in front of you, begging to be snatched up, staring you deep in the eyes, almost daring you to grasp it once and for all. The feeling you might experience in the painfully slow-approaching moments until you grab that elusive *thing* is the feeling of anxious unease I had before our first-round game against Rochester Tech.

The gym floor at the Schwartz Center was freshly lacquered and tacky, the basketballs seemed to bounce a little better than normal, the lights in the gym spotlighting us in our moments of glory seemed a little brighter than usual, and the bleachers surrounding the court were completely packed – with empty seats. The electricity in the atmosphere, in this case, came from the two teams, each preparing for a war, as for most of the players involved, this was the biggest game of our careers. In total, there may have been 10 Salem State fans in the gym that day – a few parents, my father, Sarah, and a few dedicated Viking State students, clad in orange war paint, who made the seven-hour trip to Chester, PA. Nonetheless, nothing – no lack of fan support or no amount of distance – could have put a damper on the atmosphere in that gym. I know I speak for everyone on my team when I say that on that day, we weren't playing seven hours away from home on some foreign court in front of only a handful of people. Instead, we were playing at the old Boston Garden in game seven of the NBA Finals in front of 20,000 screaming fans, each one of us wrestling with his own unique feelings of anxious unease as we all prepared to grasp the same elusive *thing*.

*****

The bus ride down to Pennsylvania was one of the most difficult rides of my life. As I've already said, I was extremely anxious to play this basketball game, and believe me, there is nothing quite like a seven-hour bus ride to let an emotion fester in the pit of one's stomach. Not even seven hours of watching comedies like Wedding Crashers, Role Models, and Tommy Boy could quell the nervous feeling in my gut.

We left late in the morning on March 5th, the day before our first-round game, so we would arrive in Pennsylvania by late afternoon for our scheduled practice time at Widener University (the host-team). The way the Division III NCAA tournament works, as opposed to the Division I tournament, is for each round, until the Final Four, the games are played at a host-team's gym. Four teams will all play their first and second round games at a host gym, in our case, at Widener University. We were scheduled to play Rochester Tech and Widener was scheduled to play Virginia Wesleyan and the two winners would play each other in the second-round game. Naturally, the host team has a distinct advantage because they will have a far more expansive fan support base than the other three teams who have to travel, in some cases, a significant distance, as was the case with us and Rochester Tech (who came from Rochester, NY). After the first and second rounds at each host gym, the highest remaining seeds become host-teams for the third and fourth rounds. For instance, if the one-seed had won its first and second round games, it would then host a third and fourth round game. (In Division I, on the other hand, every game, despite the round, is played on a neutral-site court.) If we had beaten Bridgewater State in the MASCAC championship game, we would only have had five losses and we would most likely have hosted a first and second round game.

When we finally arrived at Widener University in Chester, PA, I was astonished to see how similarly the rules and regulations of the Division III tournament followed those of the Division I tournament, mostly because almost everything else about the two levels of basketball was so different. The most striking similarity between the two divisions was the way that practices were conducted before tournament games. If our team was scheduled to practice from 4:30-6:00 p.m., that is all the time we would get in the gym. As soon as the clock struck 4:30 p.m., the scoreboard would begin ticking down from 90 minutes and when the clock hit four zeros, every player on the team had to be out of the gym and the next team was allowed to come on for their 90 minutes.

Our practice on the day before our game was as typical as ever. Coach didn't treat practice as if it were any different than any other day. We conducted our business as usual and were finished within an hour. Coach Harvey is a coach who doesn't really believe in extremely difficult practices. He's the kind of coach who believes that if you're winning and playing good basketball, practice should be for working on the little things that you can improve on as a team, rather than for running a team into the ground and punishing them or harping on the things that a team is already doing well. As the season wore on, practices became shorter and shorter time-wise, but in reality, we were just able to handle our business in a much more timely fashion and because of the shortness of practice, we were able to conserve the majority of our energy for games.

While we were in Pennsylvania, we had the opportunity to stay overnight in a hotel, something that we had done quite frequently at BC, but not a single time at Salem. While at the hotel, I roomed with Dylan, our center and team captain. (It must be something about me because I always get roomed with the center captains – John first, and now Dylan.) The hotel experience was fun, similar to the way it was at BC – at least at the beginning of my time with BC. Since the guys at Salem had never stayed in a hotel with their basketball team – or at least, very infrequently – it was a new and exciting experience (not to mention the fact that everyone was so excited for the upcoming game). While at the hotel, we did everything pretty much the same way that we did at Boston College. The first night, after practice, we had a team meal at Ruby Tuesday and then had lights out a few hours after that. The next morning we had a scheduled shoot-around/walk-through practice (just like the pre-game practices at Boston College) and after that, we had another team meal at the hotel. During our team meal, we watched some film on Rochester Tech to prepare for the game which was only a few hours away, and after the film session, departed for our first-round game against RIT.

*****

The moment the official tossed up the opening tap of our NCAA tournament first-round game, my anxiousness seemed to melt away and I was consumed entirely by the ebb and flow of the game. The first half was a back-and-forth battle, as the lead changed numerous times early in the half. At halftime, the game was still very close, as we led by a point, 34-33. At the break, the only advice Coach had for us was to keep up the defensive intensity, especially around their all-American center and the only adjustment that we made was to focus more on preventing and defending the three-ball, as for the majority of the first half, their guards were taking almost uncontested three-pointers.

As the second half began, our play became a little sloppy and we had difficulty making a shot for the first few minutes and they opened up a four-point lead, 36-40, with 17 minutes remaining in the contest. Each time they'd extend their lead past two or three I'd hold my breath, praying that they wouldn't get hot and go on a 6-0, 8-0, or 10-0 run and close the door on our season. However, that run would never come, and over the next 13 minutes, we would assemble a run of our own, going on a 37-18 tear, to take a 15-point lead, 73-58, with only four minutes remaining in the ball game, effectively closing the door on *their* season and powering us through into the second round of the NCAA tournament to face the winner of the next game, Widener, the host-team, or Virginia Wesleyan.

*****

After the game, we were so excited about our win that we didn't want to leave the gym. Our whole team stayed to watch the first half of the next game to scout the two teams. We were amazed when the Widener fans began packing the bleachers immediately upon the conclusion of our game against RIT (in fact, many Widener fans began showing up during the second half of our game). I couldn't believe the number of older people (presumably alumni) who turned out to support Widener. Apparently, there must be a huge community fan following of Widener Basketball.

Throughout the first half, I bounced back and forth between which team I would prefer to play. Widener was very similar to us – they had a very talented point guard, weren't overly big or athletic, but simply did all of the little things extremely well and moreover, efficiently. Virginia Wesleyan, on the other hand, was the type of team that I personally didn't want to play. They were very tall, athletic, and quick, however, they didn't have a whole lot of discipline or structure. Sometimes coaches use the word "raw" to describe teams like Virginia Wesleyan. Teams like that are said to have raw talent. I weighed the pros and cons in my head of playing each team and ultimately decided that it would be a tough game either way – with Widener's home court advantage and efficient basketball or Virginia Wesleyan's raw athleticism – but I decided that I'd rather play Widener because we matched up better with them. Most of my teammates took the "it-don't-matter" approach, confident that we could beat either team we played. I ended up staying to watch the entire game with Dylan and a few of the other guys and got a ride back to the hotel with my father after Widener defeated Virginia Wesleyan by eight points.

*****

The next night at 7:00 p.m., there wasn't a soul on the streets of Chester, PA. Every single person in the town, or so it seemed, had packed into Schwartz Athletic Center to watch us take on their Widener Pride. The gym was deafening as the scoreboard counted down the minutes of warm-ups. I felt far less nervous for this game and much more confident that we would get the job done. I liked our match-ups against Widener and I was excited to play in the "round of 32." (The Division III tournament starts with 60 teams, the four highest seeds receive a first round bye, and after the first round of games, the tournament field is down to the traditional 32, similar to Division I.) The players who scared me the most on Widener, contrary to RIT, were their guards. Their point guard and shooting guard were extremely quick players, both offensively and defensively. However, I liked our match-ups because we were a very guard-heavy team, too. I always felt that Stevie Celestin, our point guard, was one of the best Division III players in the country and could have guarded absolutely anyone, not to mention the fact that he wasn't stripped of the ball once the entire season while he had the dribble. Ricky and Nick were also tremendous players on both sides of the ball and I didn't think they'd have much of a problem with Widener's guards, either.

As the game opened, we began with a fire that we hadn't really had since the accident. We opened up a 5-0 lead in the opening minutes, and pushed our lead to seven, 11-4, at the 16-minute mark. They battled back behind some excellent long-range shooting, and took the lead with 13 minutes to go in the first half. I got in foul trouble early in the half and was forced to sit for most of the first half, which I wasn't happy about, but it was for the betterment of the team. My ankle had been giving me some serious trouble during the last few games and I was playing very hesitantly on it, afraid of stepping on someone's foot and rolling it again. (Actually, after the season Coach and I discussed this fear of re-injury and I have since conquered that apprehension.) The rest of the first half was a "see-saw" affair, but at halftime, we led by four, 42-38.

We began the second half with the same intensity that we opened the game with, securing a 10-point lead only two and a half minutes into the second half, behind an 8-2 run. After we pushed the lead to 10, their coach called a timeout to try to break the momentum that we had built despite only having a handful of fans. During the timeout, we were so excited that we could hardly control our emotions. Coach scolded us, reminding us that there was still a lot of basketball to be played and that Widener wasn't in the second round of the national tournament because they were lucky. He warned us that they were a very talented team and that they were very capable of battling back from only a 10-point deficit. Needless to say, Coach was right.

From the moment play resumed after that well-called timeout, Widener began chipping away at our once-thought insurmountable lead. By the nine-minute mark our lead was down to only a single point and by the three and a half minute mark, we trailed the Widener Pride by one. In the next two minutes, Dylan took over, making a 15-foot jumper and a pair of free throws to give us a four-point advantage with just 90 seconds to play. They made a pair of freebies of their own to cut our lead back to two with a minute left, but Stevie proved to have ice water in his veins as he stepped to the line with 24 seconds left and made both ends of his one-and-one. After the free throws, Widener inbounded the ball to their shooting guard, he dribbled the length of the floor, and with 19 seconds remaining, he knocked down a three-ball to make it a one-point game.

The crowd went berserk, screaming and yelling in a deafening avalanche of cheers. We inbounded the ball to Stevie and he was immediately fouled. He went back to the free throw line, the one strategically facing the Widener student section, and made the front end of his pair, but missed the second, keeping the spread at only two points. Widener secured the rebound with 14 seconds left, got the ball to their best player, their shooting guard, and he dribbled the length of the court once again with a head of steam. The volume in the gym reached an all-game high as the screams became a monotone screech and with only two seconds left, the Widener 2-guard threw up a contested lay-up from the left side which sat on the rim for what seemed like an eternity, but eventually rimmed out and escalated us into the Sweet 16!

We stormed the center of the court and celebrated, jumping and hugging one another in pure, elated ecstasy as the once-screaming crowd held its collective breath in a shocked gasp. Their inability to produce any more noise was the sweetest music my ears had ever heard; we ran off the court, fists raised in victory, under triumphant silence.

After the game, in the meeting room, everyone hugged everyone else and we celebrated as if we had won the national championship. It was the greatest basketball accomplishment of my entire life and I couldn't have been more proud to do it with the team I did it with. As we prepared to board the bus back to Salem, we learned that we would be facing Franklin and Marshall, another Pennsylvania team, and the host-team nonetheless, in the Sweet 16. We were also told that their coach was the winningest coach in Division III basketball history, but truthfully, none of that mattered. We had a week to prepare for Franklin and Marshall and we knew we would be ready. In stark contrast to the bus ride down to Pennsylvania only two days before, the return trip was remarkably restful.

Chapter XXXIX

The Sweet 16

"I was never afraid of failure, for I would
sooner fail than not be among the greatest."

- John Keats, from a letter to James Hessey, 1818

The Franklin and Marshall Diplomats were not a team that we matched up very well against. They were very deep and very big. Looking back on my year in Division III basketball, I noticed one consistent theme: the best teams were the teams that had dominant forwards and centers. Very contrary to Division I, where a true point guard with exceptional skills is very difficult to find, in Division III, which is very guard-heavy, a true power forward or center is the key piece to the puzzle and in the case of many teams, the missing cog to their machine. A nice example can be studied in our own conference, the MASCAC. The two best teams, us and Bridgewater State, each had a very dominant center, with our center, Dylan, winning the conference player of the year for the second straight year. The next level teams, Framingham State and Westfield State, each had very talented forwards, but not a true power forward or center. The next rung of teams, Fitchburg State and Worcester State, each had talented guard play (Worcester State had arguably the best player in the conference as a shooting guard), but nothing in the line of forwards or centers. Finally, the last place team in our league, MCLA, didn't have much talent at any of the three spots, and thus, went 1-24.

Franklin and Marshall, as I said, was very big. They had a true center at 6' 6" who averaged 16 points and eight rebounds per game and they also had a true power forward at 6' 7" who averaged 10 points and eight rebounds per contest. Earlier in the year, we might have been able to match up with them very well with Dylan at 6' 7" and Tommy

Henderson at 6' 8", but before the tournament started, Tommy suffered a concussion and was forced to miss the remainder of the season. Furthermore, our other power forward, Brian Clark, a 6' 5" freshman, broke his hand a few weeks before the national tournament and was also forced to miss the rest of the season. Because of our injuries, Dylan would be our only true size inside to combat the girth of Franklin and Marshall.

We did have an advantage in terms of our athleticism, as we did against almost every team we played. They had a few very quick, athletic guards, but they were very young and inexperienced, as they didn't have a single guard older than his sophomore year. We, on the other hand, had almost all junior and senior guards with a tremendous wealth of experience. If we had an advantage, it was in this area.

*****

As we prepared ourselves mentally for the opening tip of our Sweet 16 game against Franklin and Marshall, we found ourselves up against very familiar odds as in our second round game against Widener. Franklin and Marshall was the host-team and they had an extremely large contingent of fans due to their dedicated community following and thus, the gym was very loud and hostile toward us once again. Furthermore, we were faced with an issue in our team's depth, an issue we had been faced with throughout the season, but one that hadn't truly reared its ugly head until the Sweet 16 (beautiful timing, eh?). We began our season with a roster of 16 players. After only two days, we had one of our biggest, strongest forwards quit the team for personal reasons. After only a few games, one of our shooting guards decided to transfer, leaving us with 14 players. After the first semester, when grades came out in December, we were left with only 12 because Brian Marvie and Andre Beauchamp were ineligible to play for the rest of the year. A few weeks later, Zack Fahey, one of our freshmen, rolled his ankle badly coming down from a dunk in warm-ups and missed almost the entirety of the remainder of the season. Only days after Zack's injury, I sprained my ankle, too, and never fully recovered from that - physically or mentally. With the twin ankle injuries, we were down to only 10 healthy, active players. A few games later, Brian Clark broke his hand on the rim while going up for a rebound, leaving us with only nine of our original 16. Nearing the end of the season, Tommy got his concussion which left him sidelined for the remainder of the year. Finally, Nick, Bernard, and Jon were all injured in the car accident. With all that said, we only had five players who were neither injured nor suspended – Dylan, Ricky, Stevie, Dan Clark, and Tristian Shannon. With my return to the team late in the year, Nick's recovery from the accident, and Brian Marvie's return to the team for the post-season (he was able to get a grade changed and become eligible again), we had only eight players dressed and able to play against Franklin and Marshall in the Sweet 16. We had half of our original roster, including one player who had been in a car accident only two weeks before the game, one player who hadn't played since the beginning of the year, and me, who was still recovering from my injury. Unfortunately for us, our lack of depth would play a crucial role in the game against the Diplomats.

*****

The Sweet 16 game began just as the first two rounds' games had – intensely. Both teams were playing extremely quick basketball, which was our style of basketball, though it wasn't necessarily conducive to our particular situation with our team's depth in the condition that it was in. Thus, we tried to slow the tempo of the game by sinking back into a 2-3 zone defense. (A zone defense is a type of defensive alignment where each player guards a specific zone on the floor, as opposed to a particular member of the opposing team. We elected to play a 2-3 zone, with two guards at the top and the three forwards on the bottom, to try to combat their size advantage and make it difficult for their big guys to catch the ball inside.) The only problem with our 2-3 zone, however, was that because of our lack of depth, I was relegated to play one of the low spots, typically reserved for forwards. Coach usually liked having Stevie and Nick at the top of the zone because of their long arms, quickness, and aptitude to anticipate passes and steal the ball. Needless to say, life on the back line of the zone was nothing short of difficult for me. Quite frequently, I'd have to attempt to box out their center or power forward on a shot and if the ball came off my side of the rim, they could usually just leap over my back and get the ball. In reality, though, we had no choice but to remain in the zone and try to really pack it in tightly.

The first half of play proceeded, again, much like the first two games – very evenly. Our largest lead of the half was six, which we had amassed by the 11-minute mark; however, they fought back and took a six-point lead of their own near the end of the half. By halftime, the F&M lead was four; however, it might as well have been 40 because of how deeply in foul trouble we had become.

I'm not the type of player who ever blames a game on an official, nor am I the kind of player who will say an official even influenced a game. I understand that officials are as much a part of the game as the players and they can have bad games, too. With that said, however, the Sweet 16 game at Franklin and Marshall was one of the few games in my career – one of the few games I've ever played or watched – where I felt that the officials had a very key role in deciding the outcome of the game. We were playing in a hostile environment, which means referees were officiating in a hostile environment, as well. If they made a call against the Diplomats, they would hear it from the crowd. Thus, there were times in the game when an official might subconsciously not have made a call to avoid becoming the goat in the eyes of the crowd. This subconscious dilemma is something I can deal with. I've umpired baseball games and officiated basketball games and I know how difficult it is. Again, however, with that said, I felt that the extent to which these officials sided with F&M extended far beyond a subconscious aversion to becoming hated by a raucous crowd. At halftime, our three captains each had two fouls, not to mention the fact that Stevie had to sit almost the entire first half because he picked up two fouls within the first four minutes of play. (I learned later that two of the three officials who refereed our Sweet 16 game were from the state of Pennsylvania where Franklin and Marshall is a perennial basketball powerhouse and their coach is well-known and well-respected.)

We began the second half with some strong basketball, though they were able to match our intensity and built their lead up to eight points by the 16-minute mark. However, over the next two minutes, we constructed a 10-0 run and stole the lead back from them, going up by two points. Unfortunately, whether it was the referees' doing or just the fact that Lady Luck wasn't on our side that day, Dylan picked up his third foul almost immediately after we took the lead. Coach elected to keep Dylan in the game to try to build a lead; however, the plan backfired badly and Dylan picked up foul number four only one minute later. Now, Dylan, our only true line of defense against their two big bodies, was left completely ineffective because he couldn't afford to pick up his fifth foul and foul out. Immediately following Dylan's fourth foul and his forced exit from the game, F&M went on a 7-0 run and established a seven-point lead. During their run, which lasted from the 13-minute mark down to eight minutes remaining, Stevie not only picked up his third foul, but also his fourth foul, and had to take a seat next to Dylan on the bench, leaving us – already depleted – without our two best players in the game.

Over the next few minutes, their lead remained constant. Dylan came back into the game, but as I said, he was relatively ineffective. As if Dylan's and Stevie's foul trouble wasn't detrimental enough to our team, our third-best player and our third captain, Ricky, picked up three fouls in two minutes and fouled out of the game. Dylan picked up number five and fouled out two minutes later.

Entering the final two minutes of play, we trailed by six. Nicky hit a three-ball to make it a three-point deficit with two minutes to go but some timely jumpers from F&M coupled with our lousy shooting night proved their lead insurmountable and we lost the game by six points, the final score 67-61.

*****

I look back on that game and say what all members of every losing team in the history of sports have said: *"If only..."* If only we had shot the ball better. If only we had played better defense. If only we hadn't gotten into such crippling foul trouble. If only the referees had given us a fair shake. If only it had been a home game. If only my ankle had been better. *If only...*

There were just so many anomalies that night. Dylan Holmes, our best scorer and best player, shot 3-17 from the floor, scoring only six points. A player who averaged more than 18 points per game scored only six, regardless of the reason. Dan Clark, our best pure shooter, shot 1-12 from three-point range and 3-15 from the floor. A shooter who shot 40% from downtown on the year, shot only 8% on the night. (I only pick out these two players because they are both extraordinary players who simply had extraordinarily tough nights. I *absolutely* don't blame the game on them because without them, we most certainly wouldn't have been in the Sweet 16.) I was 1-2 from the floor in our Sweet 16 game for two points. 1-2 for two points. I averaged seven points per game. If Dylan makes three more shots throughout the game it's a different game. If Danny makes two more threes throughout the game it's a different game. If I score near my average it's a different game. If we have a full roster it's a different game. If we aren't in foul trouble it's a different game. *If only...*

Franklin and Marshall went on to beat DeSales the following night by 10 points, being up by as much as 18 in the second half, to advance to the Final Four. They played Richard Stockton in the Final Four in Salem, Virginia the following weekend and lost by only four points.

It makes me cringe to think of how close we were to the Final Four, only to fall short. A team that *only beat us by six points* on one of our worst nights of the season only lost by four points in a Final Four game. I feel, in my heart of hearts, that if we played Franklin and Marshall 10 times, we would beat them nine out of 10. Unfortunately, that one loss came when it mattered and our season ended March 13th in Lancaster, Pennsylvania, four wins short of the national championship.

Chapter XL

The Post Post-Season

"My responsibility is getting all my players playing for the
name on the front of the jersey, not the one on the back."

- Unknown Author

Before we played Bridgewater State in the MASCAC Championship
game, Coach Harvey delivered one of the most moving speeches I've
ever been privy to. He told us about how the night before our game, he
and his wife were laying in bed and he was having trouble falling asleep.
He asked his wife if she wouldn't mind helping him clear his mind. He
asked her to read off the names on a Salem State Basketball roster one
at a time and allow him to say the first thing that came to his mind
about each player. Word association.

As Coach relayed his story to us, tears began to well up in his eyes.
His love for us was astounding. He poured out his emotion as he told
each of us what the association was that he made with us. When he
came to me, he said, "Passion. Passion for the game. I admire your love
for the game. Anyone who could even think to leave a school like BC
for the love of the game - not to mention actually going through with it
- has a true passion that will help him succeed not only in basketball,
but more importantly, in life." My eyes became a little moist as Coach
finished with me and moved on to another player.

As I listened to the words Coach said to my teammates, I realized
that I agreed with everything Coach said about every one of them. I
realized that I loved them the same way Coach did.

His words truly touched me and I've tried to put that passion into
everything I've ever done since that day. No matter where life takes me,
whether with basketball or without it, I will always remember Coach's
words and bring that passion that he so admired.

*****

When I look back on the 2008-2009 season at Salem State College, my first thought will always be "what if?" What if we had had a better night in the Sweet 16? What if F&M had played poorly? How far could we have gone? Could we have gotten that national championship I've wanted since I was five? My second thought, however, is, and will always be, about how lucky I was to be a part of that Salem State Vikings team. I had a chance to play a Sweet 16 game in the national tournament in front of 2,000 people, including Sarah, my mother, and two of my best friends, Andrew and Crystal. I had a chance to play with some of the greatest teammates I could ever dream of playing with. I had the chance to play for a coach who welcomed me into his life like his own son and made me feel like an integral part of his team. Most importantly, however, I had the chance to live my dream. I got to play college basketball – to really play college basketball. I finally got to be happy.

I often think back to the essay that I wrote during my freshman year at Boston College (the one that begins Chapter I) and mull over the words I decided to use for the final sentence of the piece:

And in the ever-essential pursuit of perfection, in that constant strive for excellence, you will always reach the highest highs if you just surround yourself with the passion and love you have for the simple game of basketball.

These words resound in my mind truer now than ever.

PART III: Reflections on the "Road Less Traveled By"

"There is only one success – to be able
to spend your life in your own way."

- Christopher Morley, "Where the Blue Begins"

"When I was one-and-twenty
I heard a wise man say,
'Give crowns and pounds and guineas
But not your heart away;
Give pearls away and rubies
But keep your fancy free.'
But I was one-and-twenty,
No use to talk to me.

When I was one-and-twenty
I heard him say again,
'The heart out of the bosom
Was never given in vain;
'Tis paid with sighs a plenty
And sold for endless rue.'
And I am two-and-twenty,
And oh, 'tis true, 'tis true."

- A.E. Housman, "When I was One-and-Twenty"

Chapter XLI

The Importance of Education

"Education's purpose is to replace an empty mind with an open one."

- Malcolm Forbes

I remember sitting in an English literature class during my junior year at Salem State College. One day, late in the semester, when we were studying Victorian literature, my teacher asked us an interesting question: "What does your education mean to you?" While the question was simply an introduction to John Henry Cardinal Newman's *The Idea of a University*, it really got me thinking critically about what my education really means.

When I returned home from class that day, I decided to look up the word "education" to try to decipher the word's true meaning. I discovered that the word's root comes from the Latin word "ducere," which means "to lead or draw out." I began thinking that perhaps the basis of an education is something along the lines of the message expressed in Plato's *Allegory of the Cave*. In this famous work, Plato uses allegory to represent man's innate ignorance and how through learning, open-mindedness, and education, he can rise out of this ignorance (be led out of the cave) and truly drink in all of what life has to offer.

In the beginning of the work, we learn that a group of men has been chained in a cave since birth, only able to see shadows dancing on the walls of the cave in front of them. Behind them, unseen to the men, is a great fire that casts the shadows of things that move above the fire. The people also hear echoes from these moving things – animals, plants, people, etc. – and believe that the shadows on the wall are making these noises. Socrates, who is the work's protagonist, says it is reasonable to think that to these chained people, the shadows on the wall would be the realest things in their world, namely, because these are all the people have ever seen. These men do not know that their existence is "wrong" or "incomplete" and furthermore, they do not complain of their situation because they are ignorant to anything else.

Next, Socrates asks what we could expect if these men were unchained and allowed to turn around to look upon the great fire and the beings that are truly responsible for the shadows and the noises. They would be utterly confused and would not know how to name any of the beings they now look at. Furthermore, what if the freed men were forcefully dragged out of the cave and up to the surface where they can now look on the real world for the first time. Again, at first they would be tremendously overwhelmed at what they see. Some men who experience this cataclysmic change would long to return to the Cave of Ignorance; however, some will be able to accept and understand what they now see as what is truly real.

To me, these men in their initial state represent the uneducated, and moreover, they represent how I now look at a younger, less-experienced version of myself. As the men are freed from their fetters and turn to face the fire, they begin to learn new notions about what they take to be "real." At this stage in the allegory, I feel that the men are representative of me during the early years of my college experience. I had become slightly more aware of the world around me, a little more experienced, and slightly more freed from the ignorance that had kept me "chained, facing the wall" throughout the early portions of my life.

As I sit here, writing this memoir, 21 years old, I feel like I can identify with the men who have just reached the surface and are seeing the real world clearly, for the first time. When I was younger, I made decisions about what was best for me based on what I knew at the time, as I'm sure I will do when I'm older than I am now. At an earlier stage in life, I decided to go to Boston College because I knew it was a great school, I knew people would know of my accomplishments there, and I thought it would be a gateway to the medical career I thought I wanted at the time. I didn't consider any of the intangibles that I now factor into decisions quite regularly, i.e. cost, distance from home, distance from Sarah, etc. As I became more experienced, I made the decision that transferring to Salem State College was the right move. I decided that basketball was something that was very important to me, Sarah was very important to me, and a cost-efficient education was very important to me. Furthermore, as I gain even more experience in life – as the men did as they adjusted to the real world and completely rid themselves of the bonds that held them tied to ignorance during an earlier stage of their lives – I believe I will someday see the world even more clearly than I do at this moment.

So, what does my education mean to me? Ultimately, education is the guide that leads us out of the Cave of Ignorance and into the intelligible world. It is the tool that we use to break free from the fetters that hold us in ignorance and gain insight into what is really going on around us. Personally, I believe that education extends far beyond the classroom, as well. My education is ultimately the conglomeration of all of the experiences, lessons, and ideas I have encountered throughout my journey into adulthood. Whether these experiences come in the college classroom, on the basketball court, or in my daily life, each has been vital to the whole of my education – to leading me away from ignorance and toward a deeper understanding of my purpose in this life.

Perhaps the most important way my education has enlightened me is through the important discovery I made during my time at Boston College and with the Boston College Basketball team. During these two years (and eight months with the basketball program), I learned what I believe to be the truest, most fundamental, and surprisingly, most obvious reason why we should do anything in life. At the end of my time at BC, as I prepared to transfer to Salem State, I believe I was as far out of "the cave" as I have ever been in my life. With the discovery I made then, I firmly believe that I was seeing life as clearly as I ever had.

Chapter XLII

The Cultivation of Gardens

"If one advances confidently in the direction of his dreams,
and endeavors to live the life which he has imagined,
he will meet with a success unexpected in common hours."

- Henry David Thoreau, *Walden*

Remember back to my description of my first day at Salem State College and recall that I said that I was able to put into words that *something* that had eluded my reach for far too long only a few short months after coming to SSC. The ever-important discovery that I made at the tender age of 20 is simply to be happy and to live life with no regrets. Nothing in this life is worth doing if you are not completely happy in doing it. The single greatest achievement we can ever hope to obtain in life is complete and utter fulfillment – to effectuate the happiness that allows us to soar to heights previously unreachable or even unthought-of. We must grab the things in life that bring those feelings of nothing but ecstasy and elation and squeeze the life out of them until they have nothing left to offer us. For some, this *thing* is money. For others, this feeling of bliss is achieved through work, through their children's success, or through faith in an outer-world being. For others, this fulfillment may even come from basketball.

In my short, but equally significant journey through the first 20 years of my life, I had earned quite a bit. I had earned a high school diploma and a valedictorian medal. I had earned the right to attend one of the finest universities in the nation in Boston College. I had earned a roster spot on the Boston College Varsity Basketball team. I had even earned the respect of my family, friends, and peers. But to that point in my life, I had not achieved the one thing that makes everything else worth earning – I had not been completely happy for as long as I could remember. To achieve this completeness – this fulfillment – I have given up everything I have worked so tirelessly for throughout my entire life. To achieve this happiness, I have given up Boston College for Salem State. To achieve this completeness, I have chosen SSC Division III basketball over BC Division I ball. However, most importantly, I have traded the respect of my family, friends, and peers, for something greater than before – I have now achieved respect as well as admiration from these people. I have identified what it is that makes my being complete, reached out with outstretched hands and an open mind, and grasped what is mine for the taking – the state of total happiness. I believe the purpose of life is simply this: we must capture what it is that sends our minds aflutter and brings our hearts to rapturous delight, for until we are happy, we can never truly be complete.

*****

At the end of my first season with Salem State College, while stuck in rush hour traffic on the Mass. Pike during the trip back home from school, I found myself behind an old Ford pick-up truck. Proudly displayed across the back bumper was a faded sticker reading, "Live the Life you Love." I looked down at the blue and orange lettering across the front of my shirt, which spelled out Salem State Basketball, and then at Sarah who was sleeping peacefully next to me in the passenger seat of her '98 Ford Escort, and I smiled, whispering aloud to myself, "I am."